Helion & Company Limited
Unit 8 Amherst Business Centre
Budbrooke Road
Warwick
CV34 5WE
England
Tel. 01926 499 619
Email: info@helion.co.uk
Website: www.helion.co.uk
Twitter: @helionbooks
Visit our blog https://helionbooks.wordpress.com/



Front cover artwork: Two operatives of the Wagner Group posing in front of Fakhr-al-Din al-Ma'ani Castle (also known as Tadmur Castle), overlooking Palmyra in the province of Homs, Syria, in 2016. (Artwork by Pablo Patricio Albornoz © Helion & Company 2024)

Typeset by Oliver Barstow, Milan, Italy
Cover design by Paul Hewitt, Battlefield Design (www.battlefield-design.co.uk)



ISBN 978-1-804516-09-6

British Library Cataloguing-in-Publication Data
A catalogue record for this book is available from the British Library



We always welcome receiving book proposals from prospective authors.

# CONTENTS



Note: In order to simplify the use of this book, all names, locations and geographic designations are as provided in *The Times World Atlas*, or other traditionally accepted major sources of reference, as of the time of described events.

# ABBREVIATIONS AND ACRONYMS

| | |
|---|---|
| ATGM | anti-tank guided missile |
| BRI | Belt and Road Initiative |
| CAR | Central African Republic |
| CENTCOM | Central Command (of the US military) |
| CPC | Coalition of Patriots for Change |
| FACA | *Forces armées centrafricaines* (Central African Armed Forces) |
| FAMa | *Forces Armées Maliennes* (Malian Armed Forces) |
| GNA | Government of National Accord (of Libya) |
| GO | government organisation |
| GRU | *Glavnoje Razvedyvatel'noje Upravlenije* (Main Intelligence Directorate) (of Russia) |
| GSIM | *Groupe de soutien à l'islam et aux musulmans* (Support Group for Islamists and Muslims) (extremist Islamist group active in Mali) |
| IRGC | Iranian Revolutionary Guard Corps |
| IS | Islamic State |
| ISIS | Islamic State of Iraq and Syria |
| LNA | Libyan National Army |
| MINUSMA | United Nations Multidimensional Integrated Stabilization Mission in Mali |
| MOD | Ministry of Defence (of Russia) |
| NGO | non-government organisation |
| PMC | Private Military Company/Private Military Contractor |
| PSC | Private Security Company |
| SDF | Syrian Democratic Forces |
| SOCOM | Special Operations Command (of US military) |
| UAE | United Arab Emirates |
| UAV | unmanned aerial vehicle |
| UCAV | unmanned aerial combat vehicle |
| VKS | Russian Aerospace Force |
| VSRF | Russian Armed Forces |

# 1
# ANTECEDENTS & PREDECESSORS

The history of mankind includes wars from the beginning, which were waged against each other by groups of people, and later by states and empires. However, maintaining a permanent armed force imposed significant costs on those who created them, which not everyone could finance. Therefore, it was cheaper to hire well-trained mercenaries for a short period of time. It also happened that if a given country did not have enough trained armed men, they were forced to hire other armed people.[1] This soon created the institution of the mercenary, which flourished for centuries and was considered a perfectly legal occupation. Xenophon's writing *Anabasis* describes that in 401 BCE the younger Cyrus, as heir to the throne, hired 10,000 Greek mercenaries to take the Persian throne from his elder brother, Artaxerxes II. Although the operations started successfully, the claimant to the throne lost his life in the Battle of Cunaxa, so the Greeks who remained victorious on the battlefield were forced into a continuous fighting retreat to the Greek territories of the Black Sea. This book is still required reading in military schools to this day.[2]

The period between 640 and 300 BCE can be considered the heyday of Greek mercenaries, who participated in almost every major war of that period. The Egyptian ruler Psammetichus I consolidated his power in 662 BCE with the help of Greek and Carian mercenaries. The use of Greek mercenaries proved so effective that Psammetichus II also employed Greek mercenaries during his campaigns. Persian rulers also employed large numbers of Greek mercenaries; Artaxerxes hired 32,000 Greek mercenaries against the Egyptians in 380 BCE, while his successor, Darius III, hired 50,000 Greek mercenaries against Alexander the Great in 330 BCE. Several authors of the time mentioned that these mercenaries were much better equipped, trained and efficient than the armies fielded by most rulers or city-states of the day. Several clashes were decided by which of the opposing parties was able to take on more mercenaries or larger mercenary units.[3]

Italian mercenaries – known as Sileraioi or Tyrrhenoi – employed by Dionysius I, the tyrant of Syracuse (today's Sicily), in order to maintain his power, were also famous in their time.[4] Dionysius and his son Dionysius II also employed Greek mercenaries, for example in his battles against the Carthaginians, who themselves also employed Greek mercenaries.[5] A large part of the Carthaginian army was made up of mercenaries for centuries,[6] and they could have a brilliant career, such as the Spartan Xanthippus, who was also known as Xanthippus of Carthage and who won a significant victory in the Battle of Tunis in the First Punic War against the Romans.[7] Of course, it also happened that there were times when mercenaries were not paid, which could have serious consequences. Because of such a foolish move, the Carthaginians were forced to fight a bloody four-year war (the Truceless War) against their rebel mercenaries between 241–237 BCE.[8] Renowned generals such as Alexander the Great and Hannibal also employed a large number of mercenaries, who helped them to victory in several cases.[9]

In medieval Europe, due to continuous wars, the mercenary system became an institution. Wars were usually won by those who, in addition to their own armed forces and militias, were able to mobilise as many and more-qualified mercenaries as possible. Several states in the Middle Ages occasionally employed mercenaries to supplement their forces, and Byzantium employed permanent mercenary units including Normans, Turks, Italians, French, Germans, Hungarians, Georgians, Armenians, Arabs, Khazars and Slavs.[10] One, perhaps the most famous unit employed by Byzantium, was the Varangian Guard, at first composed of Rus, then Swedish, Norwegian, Danish and Anglo-Saxon mercenaries, who were primarily responsible for the safety of the emperors and their families, and occasionally

A Swiss *Reisläufer* mercenary, serving in the French Armies during the campaign in Italy during the late 1490s. (Artwork by Marco Capparoni/Helion & Co.)

engaged in military and law enforcement activities. Since they were not connected to the Greeks in any way, they could be used against the common people at any time. One of the famous commanders of the Varangian Guard was the Norwegian Harald Sigurdssons (Haardraades), who later became the ruler of Norway as Harald III.[11] Varangian mercenaries were employed in the various Russian duchies, in the Khazar Empire, and even in Hungary by several of the Árpád rulers. The Varangians not only performed bodyguard duties, but also took part in the campaigns of the Hungarian rulers, and several of them even settled permanently in the country.[12]

In the fourteenth and fifteenth centuries in today's Italy, more than 100 small and large city-states fought against each other and the papal state and since they did not have permanent high-quality armies they hired mercenaries. The leaders of these groups were known as Condottieri, and later this became the name of the system itself. The most famous mercenary leaders included Roger di Flor, Francesco Bussone da Carmagnola, Albert Sterz, Annechin Bongarden, Werner von Urslingen, Konrad von Landau, Gian Galeazzo Visconti, Ambroglio Visconti, Lodovico (or Giovanni) de Medici, John Hawkwood, Hugh de Mortimer, Miklós (or Nicholas) Toldi, Miklós Athinai, Cesare Borgia, Hannes Baumgarten, Alberigo da Barbiano, Muzio Attendolo Sforza, Gian Battista de Montesecco.[13] Among them, one of the most famous leaders was Francesco Sforza who seized power in 1447 after the death of the Duke of Milan, Filippo Maria Visconti, then made himself the Duke of Milan and founded the Sforza dynasty with the help of his mercenaries. However, few people know that even as Visconti's captain, Sforza fought together for two years and formed a friendship with the Hungarian János

A mounted Balkan *Stradiot* and an Italian hand-gunner, serving in Germany in the 1530s. (Artwork by Giorgio Albertini/Helion & Co.)

Hunyadi, who learned the 'Condottieri way of fighting' in Visconti's court. He later became one of the most successful opponents of the Turkish Empire and wrote his name in the history books as the successful defender of Nándorfehérvár (Belgrade) against the Turks. This delayed the European conquests by the Turkish Empire by 70 years.[14] However, the Condottieri or 'free companies' were not only found in Italy, but also in the service of other European rulers. Mercenaries of Italian, Flemish, Gascon, Aragonese, Navarre, Swiss, German, Breton, English, Welsh, Scottish, Hungarian, Czech and smaller numbers of other nationalities served in these units.

Famous and infamous mercenary groups included the Magna Societas Ungarorum, Catalan Grand Company, the White Company, the Company of the Star, the Black Company, the Company of the Flowers, Company of Saint George, Great Company (earlier Ventura Company).[15] In France, so-called Compagnies grandes (Breton, Gascon, English and Navarrese companies) played a similar role in the fourteenth century during the Hundred Years War.[16] Later Spanish, German and Swiss mercenaries dominated the market, but 'some Christian rulers did not shy away from employing Muslim mercenaries against their Christian opponents, despite the prohibition of the Catholic Church.'[17]

In the seventeenth century, several states established colonial companies such as the Dutch East India Company, English East India Company, Danish East India Company, French East India Company, Swedish East India Company, Ostend Company (*Kaiserliche Ostender Kompanie*) in Trieste, Swedish Africa Company and Hudson's Bay Company that actively participated in colonisation, for which they had adequate armed forces.[18] The Companies had significant autonomy, and with the exception of a few they independently decided upon and organised their activities, and the armed forces at their disposal often used violence to further these goals. In the course of their activity, they made a significant profit. For example, the armed ships of the Danish East India Company not only traded in Asian waters, but also engaged in acts of outright piracy in order to realise as much profit as possible.[19] These companies were a kind of forerunner of the current Wagner Group, which serves Russian interests in its activities.

Larger and stronger companies were often able to gain such power and independence that they operated as a 'state within a state'.[20] These companies primarily recruited officers, non-commissioned officers, and soldiers from the army of their own state, who would then serve for years in the armed forces of the mercenary companies, where they earned much more than in the regular army. Later on, if they survived, they had the opportunity to return to the regular army as professional soldiers. Of course, they could also recruit from other European countries and Germans, for example, who fought as mercenaries in almost every European war and who were employed in large numbers by the Dutch East India Company and in the colonies, were in high demand. Apart from them, Swiss, French, Polish, Swedish, Danish and Norwegian mercenaries also served in company units.[21] The various companies also recruited local soldiers such as Batavians, Malays, Sepoys, Chegos, Topasses

An Irish Galloglass, serving as a mercenary in an English army during one of the sixteenth century campaigns in France. (Artwork by Sean O'Brogain/Helion & Co.)

A 'classic' mercenary of the high medieval age: a Landsknecht of the early sixteenth century in the service of the Holy Roman Empire in Italy. (Artwork by Catalin Draghici/Helino & Co.)

and Lascorins, and after training, used them to achieve their own goals. The Dutch East India Company and the English East India Company in Asia continuously recruited mercenaries from the local population, supplemented by occasional relief troops from their allies.[22] However, the Dutch went further than that when they employed Japanese mercenaries between 1613 and 1623 to achieve their goals, who had been employed by several Asian rulers in Siam, Cambodia, and the Philippines before. Although the fighting value of the Japanese was better than that of the locally recruited soldiers, the Dutch had difficulty keeping them under control. In 1623, with the encouragement of the British, one of the Japanese units tried to take control of the Dutch fortress on the island of Ambon (today's Indonesia).[23] The French East India Company was not able to gain as much power as the English and Dutch companies, but it operated very efficiently in India as a 'mercenary intermediary organisation'. The company's officers trained smaller local sepoy units that were hired out to various rulers to fight their wars. The French were so successful in this field that the English East India Company, which was opposed to them, soon adopted and applied this method.[24]

Another change took place at the end of the seventeenth century. The mercenary companies were pushed out of the marketplace, the military units of the companies were dismissed and replaced by national forces.[25] Thus, the states monopolised violence and from then on wars took place between states.

Despite this, mercenaries were still employed in some conflicts. In the second half of the twentieth century, many newly independent African countries tried to organise their defence with units trained by their former colonisers and with the advisers and trainers they left behind. Where this turned out to be insufficient, in several cases mercenaries were hired. For example, large numbers of mercenaries served in Congo, Sierra Leone, Biafra (Nigeria), Angola, the former Rhodesia (now Zimbabwe), Comoros and Seychelles.[26] Their activities were ended by the Geneva Protocols I and II in 1977,[27] and by the international legislation adopted in 1989, which only came into force on 20 October 2001, prohibiting the recruitment, training, and employment of mercenaries.[28]

Although the institution of 'mercenary' had been officially abolished, several states needed armed groups to perform tasks that could not be performed by regular forces. This coincided with the period when the majority of states began to significantly reduce the number of otherwise very expensive armies and outsource some military/supply tasks to 'civilian' companies variously referred to as private military companies, private military contractors, military service providers, or operational contractors, for an appropriate fee.[29]

The Geneva Centre for the Democratic Control of Armed Forces (DCAF) offers the following definition of PMCs:

> Private military companies (PMCs) are businesses that offer specialised services related to war and conflict, including combat operations, strategic planning, intelligence collection, operational and logistical support, training, procurement and maintenance. They are distinguished by the following features:
> • Organisational structure: PMCs are registered businesses with corporate structures.
> • Motivation: PMCs provide their services, primarily for profit rather than for political reasons.
> PMCs vary enormously in size, ranging from small consulting firms to huge transnational corporations. Although PMCs first appeared during World War II, geopolitical changes and the restructuring of many countries' armed forces following the end of the Cold War have spurred rapid growth in the private military industry … Terms such as mercenaries and private security companies (PSCs) are often used interchangeably with PMC.[30]

Using a narrower definition of PSCs, that differentiates them from PMCs:

> Private security companies (PSC) are businesses that provide security services on a for-profit basis to paying customers. They come in a great variety of forms from small local businesses to large multinational corporations and are hired by members of the public, other businesses, and also the state … PSC can be contracted for a wide range of services, for example: as security guards, protecting people or property and regulating access to private property or commercial premises; conducting online and in-person surveillance and investigations (private detectives); improving site security through physical measures (such as locks, fences, surveillance equipment, etc.); and providing security training for state security services or other PSC.[31]

The key difference between PMC and PSC organisations is that the latter organisations may carry out limited armed activities (guarding camps, escorting convoys, etc.), but may not participate as an active combatant in a foreign armed conflict, that would classify them as mercenary.

International law covers PMCs in many ways, such as Human Rights Treaties, Criminal Law, State Responsibility (International Customary Law), International Humanitarian Law (IHL), and the Mercenaries Convention. To keep it short, we focus on two types of regulation, that is International Humanitarian Law and the Mercenaries Convention:

> IHL provides clear rules on the combat status of individual employees of PMCs, though only in cases of international and civil conflict. Like official soldiers, employees enjoy prisoner of war status if they fall under the definition of civilians accompanying armed forces. If they fall only under the definition of civilians taking part in hostilities or of mercenaries, however, they can be prosecuted by the 'enemy' state and do not enjoy the protection of normal civilians. Mercenaries Convention: The International Convention against the Recruitment, Use, Financing and Training of Mercenaries (1989) mandates that states parties have an obligation to adopt the provisions of the Convention in national laws for them to enter into effect. However, the treaty's definition of mercenary is obscure and few states have ratified it.[32]

The status of PMCs is further regulated by national laws, complicating the issue due to different approaches. Several PMCs are considered illegal by some states and legal by other states. In Ukraine, for example, all Russian PMCs are considered to be a direct threat to the national security of country,[33] while Russia has its own regulation legalising them to an extent, but also keeping them in a grey zone.[34]

These companies are connected by several threads to the governments, political and economic interest groups that give orders, and they perform tasks not only for the public sector, but also for the private sector.

Moreover, a kind of PMC boom can be observed. Governments, economic or other civil organisations are already competing to use the services of PMC organisations. PMC managers have serious political and economic connections, the ability to assert their interests, and pocket huge sums of money as compensation for the tasks they perform. A significant number of their employees were ex-soldiers or policemen, who, in addition to supply and operation activities, also performed other 'trustworthy' tasks. In this case, it is very easy to cross a limit, which is sanctioned by the laws passed by the international community, such as the aforementioned 2001 United Nations Mercenary Convention. In recent years, several countries have created PMC organisations, whose activities are not always transparent, and some of them, such as Blackwater Security Consulting (later Academi),[35] have carried out actions, such as the Nisour Square incident, that have rightly caused the international community to be outraged.[36]

In addition to them, another 45 American PMCs participated in the Iraq war, where the 25–30,000 people they employed performed vital tasks for the US units. Besides them, of course, there were also Iraqi, British, French, United Arab Emirates (UAE), South African, German, Spanish, Israeli, Czech and other PMC organisations, whose number was over 100. These organisations worked not only for the US government, but also for other organisations (GO, NGO) without committing any violations of the law.[37] But PSCs are not only connected to the US government. In recent years, China has also created several similar companies whose activities are primarily linked to the Belt and Road Initiative (BRI) program present in more than 80 countries and within which it is intended to ensure the protection of Chinese interests. These companies have not yet been transformed into full-fledged private military and security companies, and their capabilities have not yet reached those of Western or Russian PMC organisations, but they are performing more and more tasks for the Chinese government. According to a 2017 statistic, China's private security industry consisted of 5,800 companies employing approximately half a million people, and this number is constantly increasing. Only a few of these companies, barely 30, operate in an international environment, and are closely linked to the Chinese government, mainly employing former Chinese soldiers, police and members of other security organisations. Among them is Dewei Security Group Limited, which has more than 8,000 personnel in 37 countries. This organisation provides protection to China National Petroleum Corporation in Sudan and South Sudan, and for Chinese Poly-GCL Petroleum Group Holdings' Liquefied Natural Gas undertakings in Ethiopia. Huaxin China Security mainly provides protection against pirates in the Horn of Africa and in Southeast Asian waters. Guanan Security & Technology is responsible for the security of ZhenHua Oil Company operating in Iraq. According to some opinions, the weakening of Wagner could lead to the strengthening of the influence of Chinese PMCs in Africa.[38] The Gurkha Security Guards, Trident Maritime and Aegis Defence Services and, partly, the Northbridge Services Group can be linked to the British. The *Défense Conseil International* and *Groupe Geos* organisations operate in France, while Asgaard operates in Germany.[39] In addition to the great powers, other states have also established or employ PMCs. The United Arab Emirates, for example, hired hundreds of ex-soldiers and policemen from South America for serious money to use against the Iran-backed Houthis, and also deployed mercenaries in Somalia, and Saudi Arabia deployed Sudanese mercenaries in Yemen.[40] In Turkey, SADAT International Defense Consultancy was established by a retired Turkish general, Adnan Tanrıverdi, an organisation mainly operating in the Middle East region and in Islamic countries, often on behalf of the Turkish government.[41] In South Africa, several PMC organisations, such as Executive Outcomes, Dyck Advisory Group, Erinys, Ronin Protective Services, Saracen International, were established, and although the government tried to limit their activities with legislation, it achieved only minor results. Thus, South African PMCs remain among the world's most sought-after hired guns.[42] Appendix 1 shows details of some of the world's largest and better-known PSC/PMC organisations, and may be downloaded from https://www.helion.co.uk/public-downloads.php

Among these organisations, the Russian-founded Wagner Group, which is considered by more and more people not only as a simple PMC organisation, but as an instrument of Russian foreign policy, has caused the most controversy. Others go even further and identify the organisation as a modern-day mercenary group and demand that legal action be taken against them accordingly. In this study, the intention is to present the Wagner Group, the circumstances of its creation, its activities, its armed mutiny against the top Russian military leadership, the consequences of the failed coup d'état, and its possible future. It seems that a resurgent trend is being witnessed that will be even more characteristic of the conflicts of the coming decades, that those who can afford to pay for the services of PMCs will have an advantage even over states with weaker militaries.

If Yevgeny Viktorovich Prigozhin, head of the Wagner Group, was more-or-less correct, and the organisation had more than 10,000 new, mostly Russian volunteers per month,[43] it seemed certain that the birth of the largest and most capable PMC of our time was being witnessed. However, that was before the armed mutiny of Wagner, and since that time their military capabilities used in Ukraine and the income of Prigozhin were drastically cut by the Russian government. This marked the end of all sorts of pre-coup d'état analyses suggesting that most of the toughest tasks of the entire foreseeable Ukraine war would be fought by the Wagner Group,[44] that would have been an unprecedented level of PMC participation in a contemporary major war. That this is no longer the case, means that the Wagner Group exists in a very interesting, historically unforeseen stage, where not only their participation in the Ukraine war is dramatically limited by the Russian state,[45] but their future worldwide role is also called into question, including in Africa.

# 2
# FOUNDATION OF THE WAGNER GROUP

According to Western sources the Wagner Group was established in 2014 by Russian billionaire Yevgeny Prigozhin.[1] However, several Russian sources claim that the establishment in fact occurred in 2013. French sources also usually state 2014, but 2013 is also referenced. It is explained below why 2014 is the year of foundation and not 2013.

## Legal Status

The discrepancy between the dates of establishment is probably due to the non-transparent nature of the Wagner Group, and the illegal status of mercenaries according to Russian law in force at the time.[2] At least as often, the network of companies behind the Wagner Group confuses foreign observers, resulting in some sources associating its establishment with the establishment of the Moran Security Group and then the Slavonic Corps by Vadim Gusev and Evgeniy Sydorov in 2013, and link Wagner to the managers of security companies responsible for protecting commercial shipping against piracy. The three enterprises came into being in relatively quick succession: however, while the Moran Security Group and the Slavonic Corps were directly tied, their links to Wagner were only indirect by nature.[3]

While the Moran Security Group provided small teams for protection of international shipping off the coast of East Africa, the task of the Slavonic Corps was to secure selected oil installations in the Dayr az-Zawr province of eastern Syria, and it is known to have comprised 267 mercenaries. Based on poor intelligence and lots of unsubstantiated assumptions, the mission failed almost as soon as it was initiated: indeed, it failed after only one clash with native Syrian insurgents in which the Russian mercenaries proved poorly led, poorly armed, and suffered from orientation problems.[4]

All the members of the Slavonic Corps were returned to Russia, where several of them were criminally prosecuted and sentenced for their mercenary activities.[5] Gusev and Sydorov were sentenced to three years in prison because, according to the Russian law at that time, participation in armed conflicts of other countries was punishable by seven years in jail, while financing, recruiting, and training of mercenaries could result in up to 15 years in jail.

However, the majority of veterans of the Slavonic Corps were never prosecuted and that was no accident, even if Putin's apparatus of state control denied the very existence of companies like Moran and the Slavonic Corps simply because they were illegal according to its own laws.[6] Unsurprisingly, while Article 13, Paragraph 5 of the Constitution of the Russian Federation strictly prohibited the formation of armed groups, Article 208 of the Penal Code of the Russian Federation, valid since 14 June 2022 and modified again on 14 April 2023, 'clarifies' that the prohibition is for 'armed groups operating against the Russian interests.'[7]

Even more interestingly, the Russian State Duma passed a new law on 19 June 2023, allowing convicted Russian citizens to serve in the military under contract.[8] Since the official homepage of the newly adopted Russian law is inaccessible at the time this analysis was submitted, many of the details of the contract-based service of convicted personnel are unclear, such as conditions of pardoning.[9] However, it is known that those convicted due of 'serious crimes' are not eligible to serve in the Armed Forces of the Russian Federation (VSRF). Paradoxically, in the meantime, the Russian state found itself in a state of rivalry with the Wagner Group when it followed in the footsteps of the PMC by signing contracts with jailed convicts and recruiting them to serve with the VSRF.

The law of 2023 also suggest that the Russian state found the entire procedure of engaging convicted personnel in armed formations, including the military, to be 'well tested, effective and promising'. The newly passed Russian law might also suggest that at the time of its issue, the Russian state was well aware of the future role of the Wagner Group, and that the mercenaries might be forced to leave Ukraine if no new contract was signed with the Russian Ministry of Defence (MOD). Thus, it is apparent that as of 2022–2023, the leadership in the Kremlin was expecting that its enormous need for soldiers for Wagner was to be severely curtailed in the near future. The new law thus secured the position of the VSRF while also securing the position of the state, because if Wagner was ordered out of Ukraine, it would never absorb and retain all of its personnel. Finally, and in the aftermath of multiple earlier attempts to clarify the legal status of Wagner, following the armed mutiny of Prigozhin and his mercenaries against the top Russian military leadership, President Putin declared that the company was 'legally non-existent' – thus, officially, leaving the legal status of the Russian PMCs in a 'grey zone'.[10]

## THE FIRST – AND THE LAST – OPERATION OF THE SLAVONIC CORPS

Registered in Hong Kong on 18 January 2012, the Slavonic Corps came into being as a front and sub-contractor of the Moran Security Group private security company, established by Russian nationals Vadim Rudolfovich Gusev and Yevgeniy Sidorov. Its initial cadre consisted of dozens of veteran members of OMON, SOBR, Spetsnaz and the VDV, many with combat experience from Chechnya and Tajikistan.[11]

In early 2013, the Moran Security Group/Slavonic Corps began publishing job advertisements on various Russian military websites, promising US $5,000 per month for 'guard duties' protecting 'energy facilities' in Syria. The applicants were gathered in Beirut in Lebanon, before – in September 2013 – being transferred to a military base roughly between Latakia and Banias in Syria. Following a month of training and preparations, the company set up a task force of 267 men (including nine regular GRU officers), organised into two companies.

While working up the unit, many of the mercenaries realised that they had been provided with outdated equipment and could not count on support from the Russian intelligence services or the Syrian government. For example, while promised T-72 main battle tanks and BMP-1 infantry fighting vehicles, they received only one non-operational T-62. When several of the mercenaries expressed that they wished to cancel their contract, they were only offered the option to earn their ticket back to Russia through direct participation in the Syrian War. Left without choice, the Russians improvised: they began using Hyundai and GMC civilian utility vehicles and Hyundai and Iveco light trucks. Some of these were converted into 'armoured vehicles' through extensive use of thick metal plates. Many of the resulting 'technicals' were also fitted with heavy machine guns and most were decorated with posters of the Syrian dictator Bashar al-Assad. The nominal task of the unit was to travel to Dayr az-Zawr province, in eastern Syria, and secure local oil and gas fields for the duration of six months.

The Slavonic Corps went into action on 15 October 2013, when it drove in a long column down the coastal highway to Baniyas, before continuing via Tartous to Homs, and then to Palmyra. Underway along a straight road over semi-desert, they were detected by an Aerospatiale SA.342 Gazelle helicopter of the Syrian Arab Air Force. However, while trying to inspect the column, the Syrian pilot hit a power line and crashed amid the column: two of the mercenaries were injured, while others dragged the badly wounded pilot out of the burning wreckage and brought him to a hospital in Palmyra. Outside that city, the Slavonic Corps task force camped for the next two days near the local airport, which was also a forward air base of the Syrian Arab Air Force.

On 18 October 2013, the task force was put on alert and everybody ordered to their vehicles. After driving for two hours along the road to Dayr az-Zawr the column reached the western outskirts of the town of as-Sukhnah, when it was ambushed. Multiple vehicles were hit, and the mercenaries dismounted to take defensive positions, while the Cossack Company – which travelled in the rear – left the road to attempt outflanking the ambushers. Not used to the local terrain, and lacking detailed maps, the company became bogged down in soft soil. Eventually, supported by a technical belonging to the regime forces mounting an SPG-9 recoilless rifle, and several air strikes by Sukhoi Su-22 fighter-bombers of the Syrian Arab Air Force, the Russian mercenaries managed to extricate themselves from the combat zone and retreat.

Subsequently, all sorts of myths about this clash have been published in the Russian social media. Correspondingly, the Russians fought 2,000, then 3,000, then 6,000 'zealous fanatics' of the notorious Islamic State (IS), but were 'highly successful' while suffering only six wounded (two seriously) – and 'accomplished their mission'.

The actual task for which the Slavonic Corps was contracted was to secure and protect oil and gas fields outside Dayr az-Zawr. Moreover, in October 2013, the 'Islamic State' did not yet exist in the form known since 2014. At most, its presence in

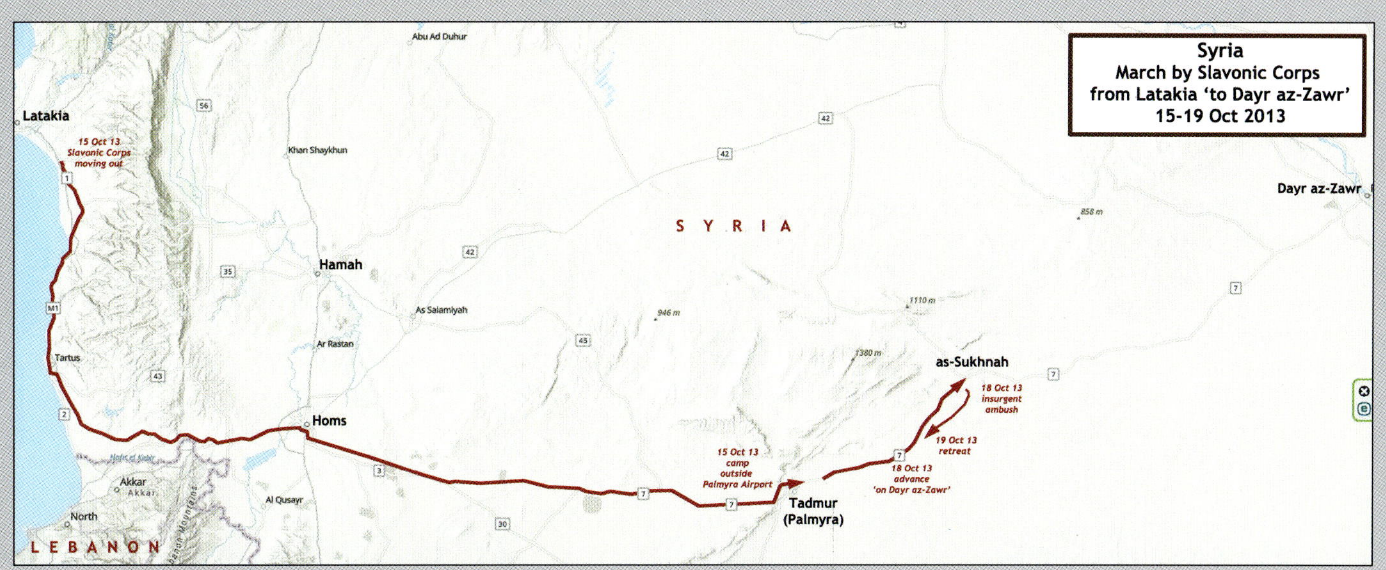


A map of the Slavonic Corps' march from the base north of Tartus, via Banias to Homs, and from Palmyra to as-Sukhna. (Map by Tom Cooper)

Syria consisted of several disparate and small groups of religious fanatics from Tunis, Saudi Arabia, Jordan and Morocco, none of which could put up more than 20–30 combatants. What the Slavonic Çorps ran into in as-Sukhna were two units of native Syrian insurgents from Dayr az-Zawr province, who had been fighting against Bashar al-Assad and his Iran-supported armed forces since 2011 and controlled most of the countryside between Palmyra and Dayr az-zawr. However, this was something nobody had informed the Slavonic Corps about. Indeed, the insurgents in question were close to surrounding the mercenary task force when a sandstorm enveloped the battlefield, limiting visibility to only a few metres. This is what saved the Russians and enabled them to conduct a relatively orderly withdrawal – not just to Palmyra, but all the way back to Latakia. The mercenaries thus never reached their intended destination.

Unsurprisingly, the appearance of the Slavonic Corps left no lasting impressions upon the local insurgents: at the least, the Russians did not prove any more effective in combat than the mix of remnants of the Syrian Arab Army and various militias controlled either by the regime in Damascus, or the Islamic Revolutionary Guards Corps of Iran, which they usually fought. Rather unsurprisingly considering the dubious outcome of the mission, the Slavonic Corps lost the contract, and all the mercenaries were returned to the Russian Federation by the end of October 2013. As far as is known, only a few 'security specialists' from the company ever received any kind of payment for their adventure in Syria.[12]

Chevrolet Silverado pick-ups, converted into so-called 'technicals' in service with the Slavonic Corps, October 2013. (Russian social media)

A column of one of the two companies of the Slavonic Corps moving out of Palmyra for its fateful march to as-Sukhna on 18 October 2013. (Wagner PMC/Grey Zone)

One of the Slavonic Corps' mercenaries with two of the Hyundai or Iveco trucks converted into armoured vehicles, seen prior to the march from Tartous to Homs. (Russian social media)

A quad 14.5mm ZPU-4 heavy machine gun of the Slavonic Corps seen in position during the clash with Syrian insurgents on 18 October 2013. (via Fontanka.ru)

## Dmitry Uktin

Dmitry Valerievich Utkin was born on 11 June 1970 in Asbest, Sverdlovsk Oblast. After graduating from high school in Smoline, he moved to Leningrad (nowadays St. Petersburg) to join the S. M. Kirov Higher Combined Arms Command School, and then joined the GRU (Main Intelligence Directorate). In early 2013, at the time he left active military service, he held the rank of lieutenant colonel and commanded the 700th Intervention Detachment of the 2nd Spetsnaz Brigade, GRU. His 'nom de guerre' was 'Vagner' – Russian for Wagner – probably because of his enthusiasm for Richard Wagner, the famous German composer. This is not where his admiration for issues related to Germany ended: according to numerous accounts, Utkin's admiration for Wagner was related to the fact that the composer was greatly admired by Adolf Hitler and appropriated by the Nazis. Indeed, gauging by several photographs, Utkin was also an admirer of Nazi Germany and had multiple Nazi tattoos, including the insignia of the *Schützstaffel* (SS).[13]

In 2013, Utkin served with the Moran Security Group, protecting ships underway in dangerous waters. In September of the same year, he then volunteered to serve with the Slavonic Corps. Once back from Syria, Utkin decided to establish his own PMC. Amid the legal vacuum on this subject, due to his links to the GRU, and with Moscow in need of a front for its designs in Ukraine, there was a 'synergy of interest': essentially, the Ministry of Defence in Moscow was keen to have a well-staffed and well-armed group on hand, which it could control at least in an indirect fashion and deploy in Ukraine while always able to exercise the option of 'plausible deniability': acting as though not having any relationship to such a group, because their sheer existence was against the law then in place in the Russian Federation. As such, this was a solution perfectly in line with the manner in which Vladimir Putin had ruled the country since the 2000. This is how on 1 May 2014 the Wagner Group officially came into being.[14]

Rather unsurprisingly, as early as 2014, Utkin and several operatives of the Wagner Group appeared in Crimea, where they operated in coordination with the special forces of both the GRU and the VSRF: known by their description as 'The Polite People Group', they were primarily responsible for the quick seizure of crucial Ukrainian military facilities and disarmament of the troops based there. Soon after, the Wagner Group was relocated to what the Russians like to call the 'Novorossiya': Donbas, in eastern Ukraine. There, they initially conducted reconnaissance operations and sabotage operations behind the Ukrainian frontlines, but also controlled supply bases, and served as bodyguards for 'very important persons.' Later, through 2014, the Wagner operatives were tasked with what was described as 'restoring constitutional order': the assassination of preposterous or selected separatist field commanders, or those that fell out of favour with Moscow. Amongst others, 'Wagner and his group' were credited with shooting the chief of staff of the 4th Brigade, Alexander 'Batman' Bednov; blowing up the commander of the Ghost Brigade, Alexey Mozgovoy; disarming the Odessa Special Purpose Brigade, and repression among 'Cossack' volunteers operating in the Luhansk Oblast.[15]

In the autumn of 2015, Utkin returned to Syria, this time in charge of a group of Wagner operatives deployed in the country. Over a year later, on 9 December 2019, Utkin then suddenly appeared in the Kremlin during the celebration of Heroes of the Fatherland Day, as a laureate of four Orders of Courage – and was promptly photographed in the company of the President of Russia, Vladimir Putin.[16]

Passport photograph of Dmitry Utkin. (via Fontanka.ru)

It was the first official, public evidence of the Wagner Group's relationship with the highest Russian circles and, immediately after, the USA put Utkin on its sanctions list, together with Concord Management & Consulting:

> The Kremlin's deniability of any formal links to the Wagner Group became famously impossible after Utkin was spotted during a video broadcast from a Kremlin reception held on 9 December 2016. After initially denying any knowledge of Utkin's existence, Putin's press secretary Dmitry Peskov ultimately acknowledged he had attended the Heroes of the Fatherland gala event at the Kremlin. Subsequently a VK (Russian Facebook) account focused on mercenary activities published a photograph in which Putin is seen standing next to four heavily – and apparently recently – decorated Wagner officers at a Kremlin function. While there is no public information on when Utkin received his latest award, a Russian website tracking military honours reported that Colonel Troshev was given Russia's highest military honour, the Hero of Russia award, plus a Gold Star order for his military services as a "volunteer" in Syria. The award was reportedly granted through a secret decree signed by Putin on 17 March 2016.[17]

Following this unplanned public appearance, Dmitry 'Wagner' Utkin was never seen or heard of in public again, and next to nothing is known about his whereabouts and actions since. According to the Turkish reports, as of late 2014 he acted only as a figurehead for the Wagner Group. Meanwhile, a growing number of sources began identifying Yevgeny Viktorovich Prigozhin as the director, and Lieutenant General Vladimir Alekseyev as the actual founder and director of the company.[18] Dmitry Uktin is known to have died in an aircraft crash on 23 August 2023, which also killed nine others – including Prigozhin. Eight days later, he was buried at the Federal Military Memorial Cemetery in Moscow Oblast.[19]

A still from a video showing three Wagner operatives during their training on RPG-7 rocket-propelled grenade launchers, at the 'Polygon' outside Moltkino. (via Fontanka.ru)

# 3
# CHRONOLOGY OF THE WAGNER GROUP

Well-connected to the GRU, supported by Lieutenant General Aleksyev, and a good organiser, Utkin and the staff led by his deputy, Andrey Troshev, worked fast: by the end of 2014, the Wagner Group – unofficially – employed up to 2,500 personnel. Most of the mercenaries were deployed in Ukraine – some in Crimea, others in Donbas – where they proved more successful than the competition in the form of the ENOT Corporation, a PMC led by Denis 'Belka' Karaban. Meanwhile, and under another contract from the GRU, another task force of the Wagner Group appeared in Syria, where it operated in support of the VSRF Group of Forces in that country.

In 2016 Wagner took an active part in the liberation of Palmyra.[1] According to Russian MOD sources, of the above 2,500 people, 1,600 were on the scene. The conclusion is that 900 people could have been in Ukraine at that time.

Until 2016, the main centre of the Wagner forces was in Molkino (Krasnodar region) within the framework of the 10th Special Reconnaissance Brigade of the GRU.[2] As far as is known, 2017 marked the first appearance of Wagner in Africa: 2,000 personnel in Libya and 300 in Sudan, though this still needs clarification.

In 2018, according to Russian newspaper *Kommersant*, there were approximately 600 Wagner fighters in Syria, while *Bloomberg News* estimated 2,000, and *Libération* 2,000–4,000 people.[3] At the beginning of 2019, Utkin moved into the background, so Wagner's African activities were coordinated by another Russian colonel, Konstantin Pikolov.[4] Utkin was distinguished in battles in Syria, later during the Crimea crisis and the Russian-Ukrainian war. However, the ownership and the financing of the Wagner Group was soon visibly taken over by Mr Prigozhin. It is most likely that the Wagner Group was founded by a businessman, and that that was Prigozhin from the beginning. On the one hand, the military leaders of the PSC, such as Utkin, were exercising their profession when leading military 'solutions', and that was the job of the fighters. On the other hand, it was the job of the businessman, especially Prigozhin, to find and maintain a relationship with Putin's inner circles within the Russian state apparatus, get the tasks from the state leadership, figure out the business interests to be served, and find resources for equipping and financing the Wagner Group. As far as is known, Prigozhin first admitted that he had been the founder of the Wagner Group only in 2022.

By March 2022, Wagner had grown to a total of 10,000 employees, of whom around 5,000 were active. Their average age was 30: the youngest was 21, the oldest 73. Wagner mercenaries came from 15 different countries, but around 75 percent were nationals of the Russian Federation.[5]

## GRU Backing

One of the principal differences between the Wagner Group and the majority of other contemporary Russian PMCs was the fact that the activities of Utkin's company were always directly facilitated by the GRU, and not merely tolerated or supported by it.[6]

Close links between the Wagner Group and the GRU were clear in matters of recruiting and training, most of which was conducted on the basis of confidentiality and personal connections. The Wagner Group strictly refused to accept any kind of serious criminal, and

Flag of the Wagner Group. (Photo by Dean O'Brien)

Black version of the Wagner PMC patch, with the slogan 'Kill them All' in Russian. (Photo by Dean O'Brien)

A typical patch worn by Wagner operatives, including the words, 'Blood, Honour, Motherland, Courage' in Russian. (Photo by Dean O'Brien)

A patch worn by mercenaries of the Wagner Group. This example shows a Grim Reaper holding an AK-47 assault rifle in one hand, while in the other he presents a business card with the text, 'Our Business is Death and Business is Good'. (Photo by Dean O'Brien)

Another typical Wagner PMC patch. This depicts a violin, and contains the text, 'Musicians which the whole world knows' in Russian. (Photo by Dean O'Brien)

A patch showing the leaders that the operatives of the Wagner Group were to look to, with images of Vladimir Putin (President of Russia), Yevgeny Prigozhin (Head of Wagner PMC), and Ramazan Kadyrov (Head of the Chechen Republic). (Photo by Dean O'Brien)

A patch showing the 'Jumbo' hand-sign, which became popular among Wagner operatives and the VSRF. It is believed to have originated from Africa, and to have been picked up by the mercenaries serving there. (Photo by Dean O'Brien)

all applicants had to undergo thorough health checks. Their training was exceptionally intense and – unlike the standard procedures for most of the Armed Forces of the Russian Federation in the 2010s – never skimped on funding. Up to 20 percent of applicants were washed out and those that failed during training received no other pay than their ticket to the training base. Discipline was strict and applicants or mercenaries not adhering to it were not only stripped of any extras, but also subjected to disciplinary actions.

Confirming the close connection between the Wagner Group and the GRU was also the fact that the main military base of the PMC was established outside the town of Molkino in Krasnodar Oblast, right next to the home-base of the 10th Spetsnaz Brigade of the GRU: indeed, the two facilities shared an entrance guarded by GRU personnel. Furthermore, Wagner operatives working abroad regularly used passports issued by the Moscow-based Central Migration Office Unit 770001 (i.e. by the Ministry of Defence).[7] The Wagner PMC made extensive use of other Russian military facilities, as well as of the military transport infrastructure of the Russian Ministry of Defence. Indeed, even the wounded of the Wagner Group were always treated in military hospitals in Rostov-na-Donu and Moscow.

Contrary to the Moran Group, which paid its mercenaries in US Dollars, the Wagner Group's rates were always in rubles: 80,000 a month were paid during training in Molkino, 120,000 for a month in Syria or Ukraine, and 180,000 a month for combat operations in either of the two countries. In the event of death, the Wagner Group promised to pay 3 million rubles to the family. Before long, the company established itself an unusually good reputation in Russia, with clear monetary calculation, no cheating, solid equipment, and good training.

The sole other Russian PMC confirmed to have enjoyed such privileges was the organisation officially termed the 'RLSPI Redut' or 'OO Redut (RCPS)' in captured Russian military documentation. As the result of an investigation with the help of several of its operatives captured in Ukraine in 2022, Redut turned out to have been a fictitious private military company: a front for GRU clandestine operations in Ukraine in (at least) 2021–2022. Perhaps unsurprisingly, although officially directed by Igor Ivanovich Shirokov, Redut never operated within the corporate network originally established by Utkin, and later by Prigorzhin: instead, its operatives were contracted by the Ministry of Defence, trained at a base outside Trigulyai, in the Tambov region, or by the GRU's 78th Intelligence Centre in Rostov-na-Donu, and deployed in combat as an element of the 3rd and 16th Spetsnaz Brigades of the GRU.[8] Unsurprisingly, and unlike the operatives of the Wagner Group, those of Redut never developed their own unifying structure or ideology, and were always directly paid by the Ministry of Defence in Moscow.

# 4 PURPOSES OF THE WAGNER GROUP

Narrowing down the capabilities of the Wagner Group, they can be identified as military and police-related elite capabilities, such as:

- storm troopers,
- field artillery (cannons, howitzers, mortars, reactive artillery [multiple rocket launchers]),
- close air support aircraft capabilities,
- cavalry (tank) capabilities,
- anti-aircraft capabilities,
- drone-related reconnaissance and strike capabilities,
- military logistics,
- military medical capabilities etc.

Based on this list of capabilities, it is clear that Wagner was far from being an ordinary PMC. References exist even concerning rare military specialisations that might justify recruiting Wagner Group mercenaries beyond the age of 50, that is a generally accepted maximum age for most applicants.

The Wagner Group's members experienced a form of elite training, closely associated with a GRU-based special forces training field in Molkino some 50km south-south-east of Krasnodar.[1]

However, since there were a huge variety of military specialisations amongst the Wagner Group mercenaries, it is right to conclude that there was non-transparent, but widely and thoroughly organised and executed, training cooperation between the Russian Military and the Wagner Group to satisfy all sorts of training, equipment and logistics needs of the PMC. This fact obscured the boundaries between the Russian State and the Wagner Group,[2] and it was not the only case. There are other cases, when boundaries between the Kremlin and the PMC were obscured, such as how high-level political decisions were made concerning where and with what purposes to employ the Wagner Group, or concerning the open-secret/hidden channels and the extent of their financing.

It is difficult to determine the number of Wagner Group mercenaries, with estimates varying to a great degree depending on the sources and the time when the estimates were published. Estimated numbers also differed based on whether they referred to the activities of the Wagner Group in particular countries or to the overall number of mercenaries engaged in worldwide activities. These figures are further complicated when the number of estimated Wagner Group casualties cannot be realistically derived from the number of mercenaries involved in operations in any given country and become part of the information warfare being waged. The authors' estimate is that the biggest Wagner Group contingent was that involved in the war in Ukraine when there were more than 10,000 mercenaries involved in military activities.

As noted in Chapter 1 'If Yevgeny Viktorovich Prigozhin, head of the Wagner Group, was more-or-less correct, and the organisation had more than 10,000 new, mostly Russian volunteers per month, it seemed certain that the birth of the largest and most capable PMC of our time was being witnessed.' With the exemption of the Russian Ministry of Defence and some powerful secret services' classified data, probably no (open) sources are credibly and precisely aware of Wagner's personnel and equipment numbers. However, there is plenty of indirect evidence, that in 2023 the Wagner Group had a significantly bigger pool of human and technical resources than ever before. Therefore, there is a need to update understanding of not only their numbers, but their role at least in the war in Ukraine. Wagner's victories in Popasnaya, Soledar and Bakhmut, successfully pushing back a contingent of 80,000 Ukrainian troops just in the Bakhmut direction, suggested that Wagner's numbers were significantly higher than previously assumed.[3]

There are top level Russian political and military decisions concerning the Ukraine war that are difficult to explain. One of them is the absence of a second wave of mobilisation following the first on 21 September 2022, when 300,000 people were mobilised, that was between 1.0 percent and 1.1 percent of the pool of roughly 25 million people having previous military experience.[4] President Putin repeatedly claimed ever since the first mobilisation in 2022, that there was no necessity to perform more waives of mobilisation.[5] Russian politicians also repeatedly claimed that the preferred way of building up the Russian Armed Forces' capabilities was to increase the number of volunteers. It should be noted that volunteers were not accounted as 'mobilised personnel', therefore their numbers compliment these. Meanwhile in Ukraine there has been a sort of 'general (full) mobilisation' since May 2022.[6] How is it possible that Russia stuck to a 1 percent 'partial mobilisation' in autumn 2022, while Ukraine has had a 'general mobilisation' since summer 2022? It is not clear even for wide layers of Russian society and that is why

The national flag of the Russian Federation with a Wagner PMC logo superimposed, consisting of a white skull in the centre of a sniper's crosshairs. (Photo by Dean O'Brien)

there have been many discussions on this topic, including claims of a 'planned' mobilisation of 1,000,000 Russians.[7]

The key to answering this question lies in the available numbers of Russian volunteers joining the armed forces. Assuming that there would be no more waves of 'partial mobilisations', and the 300,000 previously mobilised personnel could not fight indefinitely without being called home, and ultimately be replaced by others, the Russian demand for volunteers was high and constantly growing. By October 2022, more than 70,000 had signed up for participation in the 'Special Military Operations' in Ukraine.[8] Based on data provided by Dmitry Medvedev, Deputy Head of the Russian National Security Council, between 1 January and 19 May 2023, an additional 17,400 Russian volunteers signed up for military service, therefore 'the pace of the increase of the numbers of voluntary servicemen is good enough'.[9] It might be evident, that whoever signed up voluntarily to join the Russian Armed Forces in the middle of the Ukraine war, could easily find themselves as a participant in that war. It might be a conclusion, that those volunteering to join the Russian Armed Forces, in circumstances of a high probability of fighting a major war, were also tempted to join Wagner for several reasons, such as much more significant payment and professional training, for example.

## Wider Purposes

Essentially the Wagner Group was a Kremlin-backed PMC, owned by Prigozhin and financed by the Russian Ministry of Defence. However, as a tool of promoting Russian influence in many countries, its purpose extends far beyond security.[10] Its role includes political and economic influencing. Since the Wagner Group by itself does not officially represent the Russian government, they in fact operate in a sort of a grey zone. Thus, they can be viewed not only as a tool, but also as an extension of Moscow's influence providing opportunities of doing business where official Russian government presence is undesired for a variety of reasons. Such reasons could be some extremely dangerous military operations, biased election monitoring, support of partially or entirely illegal businesses, and various forms of support for autocratic regimes, including the liquidation of politically adverse forces.

## The Love and Hate Affair with the Ministry of Defence

In 2023, by when the importance of the Wagner Group had grown by an order of magnitude, nobody less than Sergey Shoygu, Minister of Defence since 2012, appointed Army General Sergey Surovikin to the position of a 'Chief Coordinator' between the MOD and the Wagner Group.[11] The qualities and status of General Surovikin and an analysis of his role influencing the fate of Wagner will be returned to later.

It might also be evidence of Wagner's former importance for Russia in Ukraine, that Sergey Shoygu also appointed the three-star General A. Kuzhmenkov to be specifically responsible for weapons and ammunition supply to the Wagner Group. In early May 2023 the group claimed serious supply issues, threatening the Russian Ministry of Defence with a complete troop withdrawal from Bakhmut by 10 May 2023.[12] That was the day following the Russian

Entrance to the headquarters of the Wagner Group in St. Petersburg, photographed in late December 2022. (Photo private collection)

The revolving doors at the entrance to the headquarters of the Wagner Group, displaying the organisation's corporate logo. (Photo private collection)

Victory Parade celebrating victory in the Great Patriotic War, considered to be a most important occasion for the Russian state and the Russian people. Therefore, Prigozhin's statements could be viewed by the Russian public both as betraying Mother Russia, and also as a desperate claim to change previously established Russian practices in supplying the Wagner Group.

There is also lots of evidence, at least on the surface, that there was a serious rivalry between the Russian MOD and the Wagner Group. The question is whether it was a misleading show for the consumption of foreign observers – in style of the classic Russian *maskirovka* – or whether this was a serious issue. There were signs suggesting that it was both.

Russian MOD officials and high-ranking military officials commanding Russian troops in Ukraine were likely to hate Wagner for its successes, seeing the PMC as a rival. On the other hand, in a time of fierce information warfare fought in part via social media – where Wagner troops might have suggested that they were less capable than they really were to encourage a Ukrainian counteroffensive – any public dispute may have been a fake news story. Should a Ukrainian counteroffensive fail, Kyiv might lose most of its reserves in terms of manpower and military assets, paving the way for a successful Russian offensive. Meanwhile, such a situation might convince Ukraine's Western supporters to seriously decrease their support to Kyiv in the absence of military success and growing costs on their side.

As the popularity of the Wagner Group grew, so also its 'merchandise' became more diverse. This neck warmer carries the group's insignia. (Photo by Dean O'Brien)

A souvenir mug, showing the Wagner insignia, based on the original Soviet-style mug used by the Red Army during the Great Patriotic War (1941–1945). (Photo by Dean O'Brien)

# 5
# MUSICIANS AROUND THE WORLD

The Russian military intervention in Syria was launched in August 2015, at the invitation of the regime of President Bashar al-Assad and his primary supporter, the Islamic Revolutionary Guards Corps (IRGC) from Iran. Its primary purpose was to save the Assad regime from collapse.

## First Tour

The presence of the second group of Russian mercenaries in Syria can be traced back to the autumn of 2013, when a team or two – a total of about 40–50 operators – was contracted by the Cypriot offshore company Zeitplus Consultancy Services Ltd, the president of which turned out to be Igor Borisovich Tolstoshein, an oligarch from St. Petersburg. According to contemporary reports, their task was to guard military warehouses near Damascus and serve as bodyguards in that country, and in Lebanon, for a period of six months. Unlike the mercenaries of the ill-fated Slavonic Corps, the mercenaries of Zeitplus remained in Syria for much of 2014 and only a few returned to Russia in early January 2014 amid disagreements about financial arrangements and 'immoderate…consumption of alcoholic beverages'.[1]

Arriving in Syria in October 2015, the first team of Wagner troops was therefore only the third Russian PMC to operate in the country. Their initial task was that of training, advising, and providing logistical services for the pro-Assad forces. Subsequently, this was expanded to intelligence-gathering, and then to actual military operations.[2]

Because the latter brough the Wagner PMC to the scenes of some of the most intensive warfare in this conflict, the contingent was rapidly expanded to around 2,000–2,500 men, equipped with T-72 tanks, BPM-97 Vystrel armoured scout cars, Ural-432007 Shchuka mine-resistant, ambush-protected (MRAP) vehicles, BM-21 Grad multiple rocket launchers, 122m D-30 towed howitzers, 23mm ZU-23 automatic anti-aircraft guns, and lots of machine guns – all provided by the Russian Ministry of Defence. Additional BRDM armoured scout cars came from the stocks of the Syrian Ministry of Defence. While there is no precise information about the exact composition of the contingent in question, it is certain that it included the following elements:

- a command group
- four reconnaissance and assault companies
- a tank company
- a combined artillery group
- reconnaissance and support units.[3]

According to several experts, Wagner's effectiveness significantly exceeded that of the better equipped and supplied, but under-

A group of Russian mercenaries pose during their deployment in northern Palmyra province in Syria. (Novaya Gazeta)

A Vystrel armoured reconnaissance car seen in the Palmyra area in 2018. (Wagner PMC/Grey Zone)

motivated and untrained forces loyal to Bashar al-Assad. Nevertheless, the Russian mercenaries suffered significant losses – which Moscow kept strictly secret. This proved far from easy because the presence of Wagner mercenaries could not be kept secret as ever-more Russians realised that although it was forbidden to serve as a mercenary in Russia, they could earn significant sums of money by joining the group, while others were keen to do so for motives of nationalism. [4] The Wagner Group was deployed in Syria under a contract from the Russian Ministry of Defence and thus nobody had to fear possible prosecution on returning to the Russian Federation. In turn, the Kremlin had a constantly growing interest in employing ever-more mercenaries because by doing so it was preventing the possible deaths of regular VSRF troops in Syria.[5]

According to official statements, the Russian army suffered a loss of just under 100 servicemen during its several years of operations in Syria.[6] Although this number is hard to believe, it is certain that without Wagner's gunmen, this number would be much higher.[7] It must be kept in mind that the number of mercenary casualties suffered by the Wagner Group did not have to be accounted for to Russian society, since they did not officially exist. Of course, the 'rent/salary' of the organisation's armed forces had to be paid, but this was more acceptable than possible social dissatisfaction due to the death of Russian soldiers, as a result of which some military leaders might be demoted, transferred, or even fired. In addition, the Russian Ministry of Defence provided continuous logistical support to Wagner, which was constantly engaged in combat.[8] Almost immediately after its arrival, the organisation was confronted with the deadly effectiveness of ISIS (Islamic State of Iraq and Syria) militants. In October 2015, the Wagner Group's Nabi Younis base in western Syria (Latakia) was attacked, in which at least seven mercenaries lost their lives.[9] In December of the same year, the members of one of the reconnaissance units wandered into a mined area, where one of the scouts lost his life. In addition, there were further losses which were confirmed by security expert Denis Korotkov and other sources. According to Korotkov, 93 Russian mercenaries went to Syria in September 2015, two-thirds of whom were killed or wounded by the end of December. Not only Russians served in Wagner's ranks, but also mercenaries of other nationalities, the largest number of them being Serbs who created an independent platoon under the leadership of Davor Savicic, who had earlier served together with Utkin in the ranks of the Slavonic Corps.[10]

## THE FIRST WAGNER MERCENARIES IN SYRIA

Officially at least, President Vladimir Putin launched the Russian military intervention in Syria in August 2015, in response to an invitation from the President of the Syrian Arab Republic, Bashar al-Assad. The actual situation was significantly different.

Since facing a popular uprising and then an armed mutiny within its armed forces in 2011, the Bashar regime defined its legitimacy through the level of control it exercised over the major urban centres of Syria. Therefore, when facing mass-demonstrations by civilians, followed by an armed mutiny within its armed forces, it launched a campaign of mass arrests while attempting to prevent the dissolution of the Syrian Arab Army through corseting loyal elements of its 20 divisions through their subordination to elements of different intelligence and security agencies. Nearly all of the operations of the resulting 20 task forces failed and these units suffered heavy losses and began to disintegrate. The regime therefore reorganised its forces once again and deployed them to guard over 2,000 different checkpoints around major cities. Rather unsurprisingly, this completely destroyed the cohesion of the armed forces and by October 2011 the regime was not only on the verge of defeat but also financially bankrupt.

At that point in time, the leadership of the IRGC decided to prevent the collapse of the regime in Damascus and in November 2011 launched a military intervention in the country. At the time, Tehran was engaged in negotiating with Western powers for the Joint Comprehensive Plan of Action – primarily related to Iran's nuclear program – and thus the government of the Islamic Republic of Tehran was not only concerned about spoiling the talks, but also about a possible Western counter-intervention. Therefore, the IRGC acted clandestinely: while it deployed two small brigades of troops to Syria, its primary task was that of reorganising whatever was left of the armed formations still loyal to Assad. Keen to maintain as minimal a footprint as possible, the Iranians did so through the creation of numerous militias, all officially established as a part of the National Defence Force. Led either by Assad's henchmen or local favourites and bolstered by the IRGC units and IRGC-controlled units of Hezbollah from Lebanon, these bore the brunt of fighting for the next three years. Although Tehran spent over US $100 billion, by mid-2015, Assad and the IRGC were in danger of losing the war. Therefore it was decided to invite a Russian military intervention.

Because by August 2015, the insurgents were advancing on the port of Lattakia, and because Moscow was uncertain about a possible Western reaction, the operation was initiated in a great hurry, conducted clandestinely, and poorly planned. The essential idea was to deploy a regiment-sized formation of the Russian Aerospace Forces (VKS) to Hmeimim (or Khmeimim) Air Base in Syria, and to bomb the rebels to a standstill by use of air power alone. However, to secure this base, to rebuild all the disparate militias created by the IRGC and reform them into a coherent armed force, while also safeguarding Assad's regime from Tehran's designs, the Russians required the presence of their own troops. This idea was also useful for Putin, who was searching for an opportunity to get rid of the many witnesses to the direct Russian involvement in the invasion of Ukraine and Donbas a year before. This is how it came to be that the first group of Wagner mercenaries arrived in Latakia in late August 2015, at around the same time as a battalion tactical group of the 810th Naval Infantry Brigade also appeared there. Their initial task was to secure Latakia through advising, training and reorganising a group of Alawite militias active in the area north of the city, in turn helping secure Hmeimim AB.

## Second Tour

In February 2016, President Putin declared the Russian military intervention in Syria to be complete and announced the withdrawal of the Russian Group of Forces. At least officially, a significant contingent of the Russian forces was withdrawn back to their bases in the Russian Federation. Actually, most of the VKS aircraft and the first few battalion tactical groups of the VSRF to reach the country were rotated out, and replaced by similar-sized contingents of fresh troops.

The Wagner operatives left the country in summer 2016. However, by then it had become obvious that the war in Syria was not over. Indeed, although the Russians helped Syrian and IRGC forces to push the insurgents away from Latakia, and to lift the sieges of two predominantly Shia villages north-west of Aleppo, the war went on. Indeed, aiming to recover 'every square metre' of Syria, the IRGC and the Assad regime felt emboldened to continue their own offensives. In similar fashion, the insurgency, supported by Turkey and Qatar, aimed to recover not only the ground they had lost in northern Hama, but also to complete the conquest of Aleppo. Finally, for its part, the Islamic State was aiming to complete the conquest of Aleppo Province in the north, and to drive in the direction of Damascus in the south.

Unsurprisingly, only weeks after its withdrawal, the Wagner Group was recalled to Syria. Compared to its first deployment in the country, reportedly, the second one was undertaken under less favourable conditions. This time, the Russian Armed Forces were not present in similar numbers, nor ready to provide a similar level of equipment and logistical support as in 2015. Moreover, the Wagner Group was forced to conduct combat operations more often and as a result its mercenaries suffered significant losses.

On the other hand, during its second stint in Syria, the Wagner Group was ever less willing to hide its presence. As more of its operatives were killed, their funerals were attended by representatives of the armed forces – in turn attracting the attention of not only the relatives and friends of the fallen, but also the representatives of the Russian and international press. Although various investigative journalists and portals discovered the identity of several fallen mercenaries, the Russian government strongly protested whenever their possible connection with the organisation was investigated.[11]

This also happened in September 2017, when the Islamic State launched a counterattack near the city of Dayr az-Zawr, where the terrorists captured two Wagner mercenaries, Grigoriy Tsurkanu and Roman Zabolotniy. The Kremlin strictly denied any connection with the captured Russians and nothing was done to rescue them. It is not known whether the management of Wagner tried to free the hostages or offered a ransom for them. In any case, they contacted the parents of Grigoriy Tsurkanu, who they claimed would save the boys, but later only confirmed the news of his death.[12]

During its second tour in Syria, elements of the Wagner Group were involved in three battles for Palmyra against IS in 2016 and 2017; in operations in reaction to the insurgent counteroffensive into northern Hama in 2017; and in the offensive aiming to lift IS's siege of Dayr az-Zawr later the same year. Of other tasks assigned to the Wagner Group, the most important was the training of several pro-Assad militias. The most prominent of these became the group known as the 'ISIS Hunters'. Established in early 2017, after forces loyal to Assad were routed in the Second Battle of Palmyra, and after a reported coup attempt in Damascus staged by the IRGC, this unit was entirely composed of volunteers trained by Russian mercenaries. Although famed for its 'achievements' in combating IS,

Russian mercenaries with a BMP-1 infantry fighting vehicle in the Palmyra area in 2017. (Wagner PMC/Grey Zone)

Due to the poor condition of vehicles acquired from stocks of the Syrian Arab Army, in 2017 the Wagner operatives in Syria began acquiring Chekan and Shchuka MRAPs, based on the chassis of Ural 4320 trucks, from Russian production. The vehicle proved much easier to maintain and operate but also offered poorer protection from enemy firepower when compared to Syrian vehicles. (Wagner PMC/Grey Zone)

A group of Russian mercenaries on a march in the Palmyra area in 2017. (Wagner PMC/Grey Zone)

it remained a relatively small unit: at most consisting of around 200 mid-aged combatants, the primary purpose of which was to serve as a counterweight to numerous militias controlled by the IRGC.

In 2018, the slow growth of the ISIS Hunters eventually led to the idea to create the V Assault Corps, as a Russian-equipped and -trained unit, largely consisting of reorganised militias loyal to Assad, but also of former insurgents pardoned under several amnesties offered in the meantime. Both of these forces were deployed during the fighting in the Aleppo area in late 2017 and early 2018, and then to Dayr az-Zawr – where they not only fought IS, but also the US-supported Syrian Democratic Forces (SDF).[13]

## ORGANISATION CHART OF THE WAGNER GROUP IN SYRIA IN 2017[14]

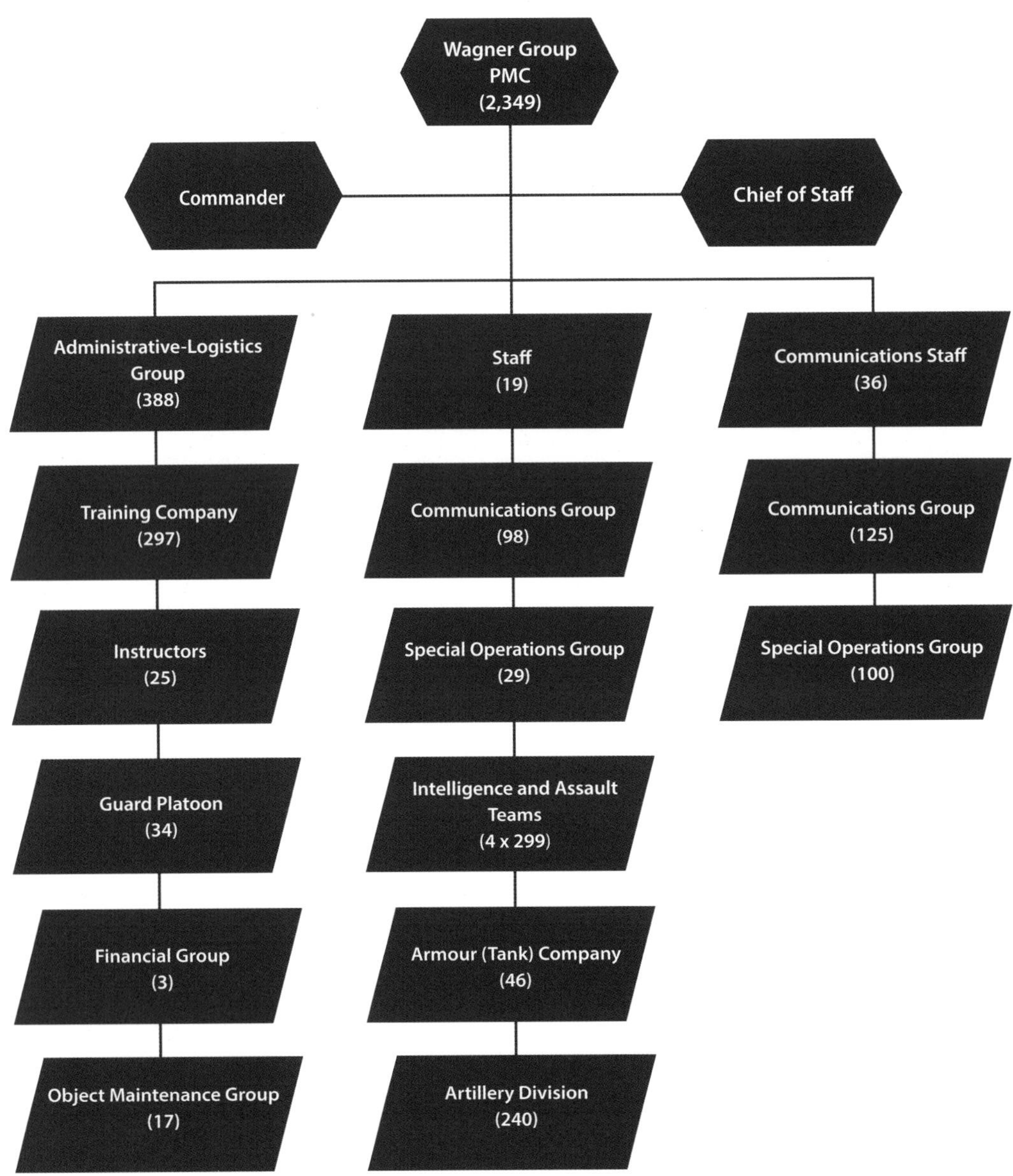


### Atrocities

In July 2017, a scandal related to Wagner operatives erupted when it became known that several of them had brutally tortured and executed a Syrian soldier who wanted to desert, and had recorded the atrocities in two videos.

In 2017, Denis Korotkov, a journalist for *Novaya Gazeta*, received a video showing a local person being tortured by Russian-speaking soldiers in unmarked military uniforms. All of this happened in the area of the Jihar Gas Facility (Al Shaer gas field), which was supervised by Wagner. In this first video, no one could be identified other than the victim Muhammad Taha Ismail Abdullah, more commonly known as Hamadi Bouta, who was identified by his brother on the basis of the video.[15] Three months after the first video, a second one appeared on the internet, in which it can be seen that the victim's head was cut off with a knife, then his body crucified in the shape of an X, and set on fire.

In the autumn of 2019, Korotkov received another video of the torture in Syria. This time, however, one of the participants had his face uncovered. Korotkov ran facial recognition software on the Russian social networking site VK (*VKontakt*) and based on the picture he managed to identify Stanislav E. Dychko, a former policeman born in 1990. It turned out that the victim was a deserter from President Bashar al-Assad's forces, who had also worked with Wagner PMC in the past. Korotkov found out that the direct order to the torturer was given by Utkin, who was presumably very annoyed by mass desertions from Wagner and that the scene was filmed because they wanted to set an example. They filed a complaint in court, but the video was not legally accepted as evidence by the Russian court. Korotkov subsequently received threats to his life, including via online groups where people were encouraged to kill him, and became one of Prigozhin's main enemies. Dychko changed his name, undertook no more Wagner missions, and died in July 2021, perhaps executed.[16] For this, as well as for other similar actions

By 2018, the Russian mercenaries in Syria were operating a number of heavily modified BRDM-2s. Visible behind the combatant here are an example mounting an AGS-17 grenade launcher, and in the background, one mounting a remotely-controlled ZU-23-2 automatic anti-aircraft gun. Note the additional bar armour on both vehicles. See colour section for additional details. (Wagner PMC/Grey Zone)

Another heavily modified BRDM-2, mounting a remotely-controlled ZU-23-2 automatic anti-aircraft gun, on a barge carrying it across the Euphrates River in early 2018. (Wagner PMC/Grey Zone)

in Ukraine, Libya, the Central African Republic (CAR), Sudan and Mozambique, sanctions were imposed on several people at Wagner, including their founder Utkin.[17]

## Battle of Khasham

Meanwhile, in December 2016, a delegation of the Syrian Minister of Oil and Gas, Ali Ghanem, visited Moscow, where he was received by the Russian Minister of Energy, Alexander Novak. An agreement was signed between the Syrian National Oil Company on the one hand and on the other, a Russian company newly created in St. Petersburg, Europolis LLC (or Euro Polis LLC). This company had committed itself to fight for the liberation of the oil and gas fields in Syria, and to protect the fields, in return for 25 percent of the royalties from the production.[18] Immediately after, Europolis signed a contract with Prigozhin's Wagner.[19] Correspondingly, immediately after concluding the offensive that lifted the siege of Dayr az-Zawr, the Russian mercenaries in Syria were reorganised and deployed to protect the oil- and gas fields between that city, Palmyra and Homs.

In November 2017, the Kremlin announced that the Russian military intervention in Syria had been concluded – once again – and that it would start withdrawing its troops from Syria. Indeed, on 11 December 2017, Russian President Vladimir Putin went as far as to visit the Russian air base at Hmeimim in Syria, publicly announce victory over the Islamic State, and the beginning of the withdrawal of Russian troops.[20] Russia did not actually give up anything of its ambitions in Syria: therefore, Wagner and a few other Russian security companies had to assume a significant part of the previous tasks of the armed forces.[21]

In need of bolstering its numbers and thus improving the security of the area between Dayr az-Zawr, Palmyra and Homs, in the second half of 2017 the Wagner Group began hiring local Syrians. Concurrently with its recruiting campaign, the Russian propaganda machinery began circulating reports about 'massive reinforcements' of Assadist and Russian forces deploying to the Dayr az-Zawr area, and an 'agreement' with the US and the PKK/YPG/SDF for these to assume control of the Taibye oilfield (also known as the Conoco), east of Dayr az-Zawr, on the left bank of the Euphrates River.

Actually, the only force loyal to Assad present in the area at the time was that of Liwa al-Bakir: an IRGC-controlled militia of Syrian Shia. Supported by the Wagner Group, Liwa al-Bakir recruited enough local Sunnis to establish three small battalions: one each for the villages of Mazlum, Marrat and al-Hatlah. All were declared to be part of the 'National Defence Force' and were trained with the help of the Russian mercenaries and equipped with arms drawn from Assad's arsenals. Liwa al-Bakr was followed by a brigade of the Liwa Fatimiyoun: a division-sized, IRGC-controlled unit consisting of up to 20,000 Afghan Hazaras – all children of refugees from Afghanistan, recruited in Iran in return for receiving citizenship. Finally, by late January 2018, elements of the notorious 4th Armoured Division also began appearing in the area: a formation officially commanded by Maher al-Assad, Bashar's brother and the crucial linchpin in cooperation between Damascus and Tehran.

While this build-up, recruitment of members of the Bakara and al-Bohamad Arab tribes, and their training were going on, the Syrian Ministry of Oil and Gas attempted to enter negotiations with the SDF. However, the PKK-controlled organisation refused to accept any kind of deal. Eventually, the IRGC – probably encouraged by Prigozhin – lost patience and, at around 05.00hrs on 7 February 2018, ordered its units to start crossing the Euphrates River on a pontoon bridge located south-east of Dayr az-Zawr. Warning shots by US special forces operatives deployed nearby, brought this deployment to an early end, and the Liwa al-Bakr combatants withdrew west of the Euphrates.

At around 22.00hrs on 7 February 2018, about 200 IRGC-controlled combatants then crossed the Euphrates again and marched in the direction of Khasham. At the same time, another element of either Liwa al-Bakr or the 4th Armoured Division moved on Tabiyet Jazira, a village controlled by the Syrian regime. The IRGC commanders announced to the Syrian combatants that they were about to attack an 'IS sleeper cell'. The initial moves were actually a show of force, aimed at impressing the SDF enough to cause them to withdraw from the area of interest.

However, the leadership of the PKK/YPG/SDF conglomerate was not impressed. Instead, it requested help from US special forces operators accompanying its troops in the area, and in turn these called for help from CENTCOM (Central Command of the US Armed Forces) and SOCOM (US Special Operations Command). CENTCOM had been monitoring the build-up of what Washington termed the 'pro-Syrian regime' forces in the area east of Dayr az-Zawr for at least a week, and thus was aware of the IRGC preparations for an attack. Moreover, they had intercepted a communication between Prigozhin and Mansour Fadlallah Azzam, a senior official in the Assad regime, in which the Russian boasted he had 'secured permission' from an unspecified Russian minister to 'go ahead with a fast and strong move' in early February, and was waiting for approval from Damascus.[22] Indeed, the Americans went as far as to warn the headquarters of the Russian Group of Forces in Syria via the telephone deconfliction line, well before anybody made the first move. However, to no avail.

Therefore, when Liwa al-Bakr approached Khasham, CENTCOM and SOCOM reacted relatively quickly and in a particularly vicious fashion. After communicating with the headquarters of the Russian Group of Forces in Syria at Hmeimim Air Base, to make sure that no elements of the Russian Armed Forces were involved, they ordered all available assets into action.

While the Americans were gearing up, the three newly-established battalions of the IRGC's Liwa al-Bakr approached Khasham. Their first attack hit the SDF hard and achieved significant success – until elements of the US Marines and Green Berets intervened: their superior firepower stopped the assailants. In turn, the IRGC deployed several T-72 main battle tanks, supported by mortars and light artillery.[23] The Americans hit back with General Atomics MQ-9 Reaper UCAVs (unmanned aerial combat vehicles) and systematically knocked out the artillery and tanks with the use of AGM-114 Hellfire anti-tank guided missiles.

Meanwhile, the omnipresent communications and signals intelligence of the US armed forces intercepted several radio messages from the battlefield area in the Russian language. CENTCOM contacted the Russian headquarters at Hmeimim again, enquiring if any members of the Russian Armed Forces were present within the combat zone. When Hmeimim categorically denied that Russian forces were present, the US forces unleashed their air power: in a series air strikes that went on for hours, Boeing F-22 Raptor and Boeing F-15E Strike Eagle fighter-bombers and Lockheed-Martin AC-130 gunships of the US Air Force, General Atomics MQ-9 Reaper UCAVs, as well as Boeing AH-64 Apache attack helicopters of the US Army, together with the artillery of the US Marine Corps (comprising a battery of M142 HIMARS multiple rocket launchers), subjected the assailants to murderous volumes of high-explosives.

Unsurprisingly considering the IRGC and the commanders of its militias in Syria never expected, nor had ever before experienced

A still from a video taken by a US-operated UAV, showing a group of around 12 combatants around an M1928/M30 122mm howitzer deployed in Khusham, seconds before it was hit and completely destroyed. According to several unofficial Russian sources, this was the moment numerous Wagner operatives were also killed. (CENTCOM)

this kind of opposition, or were equipped to counter this kind of enemy, the results were devastating. According to subsequent reports from the Pentagon and the SDF, at least 100 'pro-Syrian regime' combatants were killed. Unofficial Syrian sources reported up to 150 casualties – including 61 fatalities (amongst them 25 'members of local tribes'), while Nidal Gazaui, an SDF spokesperson, added that the attacking force consisted of more than 500 troops, and lost more than 20 vehicles, including nine main battle tanks. However, much of the foreign media then began spreading stories originally published by unofficial Russian sources about '20–30, 65, 218….300 Russian mercenaries killed' – although there was no doubt that the US forces were fighting an IRGC-controlled force largely consisting of Syrian nationals, and there was next to no evidence of Russian involvement.[24]

Although it is near-certain that at the least a group of Wagner operatives serving as instructors to Liwa al-Bakr became involved and was hit by the US forces, the exact number of Russian mercenaries killed or wounded remains unclear. What is certain is that a group of between 10 and 20 was deployed in the village of Tabiyeh: although not directly involved in the fighting, they were targeted by the US forces, which continued pounding the IRGC-controlled formations through the morning of 8 February and the following day, even when these merely attempted to retrieve bodies of those killed in earlier fighting. Only on 17 February was Andrei Troshev, one of the directors of the Wagner Group, able to officially announce that 14 (Russian) 'volunteers' died in the battle.[25]

Wreckage of a ZSU-23-4 Shilka self-propelled 23mm anti-aircraft gun, from either Liwa al-Bakr or the 4th Armoured Division, destroyed by US firepower during the battle of Khasham. (Syrian social media)

A 2S1 Gvozdika self-propelled howitzer of the 4th Armoured Division, knocked out by US firepower during the night of 7 to 8 February 2018. (Syrian social media)

During this clash, The Group of Russian Forces in Syria did scramble several of its fighter-bombers from Hmeimim AB. One of these approached the combat zone, but turned away without engaging: neither the Kremlin, nor the military leadership in Syria was ready to risk a direct conflict with US armed forces.[26]

## The Drawdown

In exchange for keeping the Assad regime in power, Russian companies (Europolis for example, owned by Prigozhin) acquired oil, natural gas fields and mines in the country, which were also guarded by the Russian PMC. Originally, 3,000 mercenaries served in the country, whose number exceeded 5,000 in 2018, among whom were Chechens and Ings, and later Syrians.[27] For its activities, Wagner obtained oil and gas concessions, the income of which paid the salaries of the operatives, financed acquisition of additional arms and ammunition, and supported various other Russian goals. This became an important issue because the management of the Wagner Group soon came into conflict with the Russian Ministry of Defence, which first reduced, and then eliminated all the financial and logistical support provided to Wagner, so the organisation had to develop a 'self-sustaining model'.[28] It was then that the previous uniform salary was abolished and those serving in combat formations and reconnaissance received a higher salary than mercenaries performing other supporting tasks (guarding and protection, logistical support, operation of drones, etc.).[29]

This type of financing system, known as the 'Syrian model', worked so well that it was also used in African countries, where Wagner subsequently became involved in numerous 'business activities', in addition to providing its usual services.[30]

An operative of the Wagner Group in the hills of the Palmyra area in 2017. (Wagner PMC/Grey Zone)

Two Russian mercenaries with a Patriot SUV, mounting a 14.5mm Dushka heavy machine gun, in the Dayr az-Zawr area in 2017. (Wagner PMC/Grey Zone)

Left to their own devices, the mercenaries of the Slavonic Corps deployed in Syria in 2013 were forced to improvise. Amongst others, they acquired a number of Chevrolet Silverado pick-ups and fitted these with a pedestal for a light machine gun, and had their engine, front of the cabin, and the sides protected by simple (and rusty) steel plates. (Artwork by David Bocquelet)

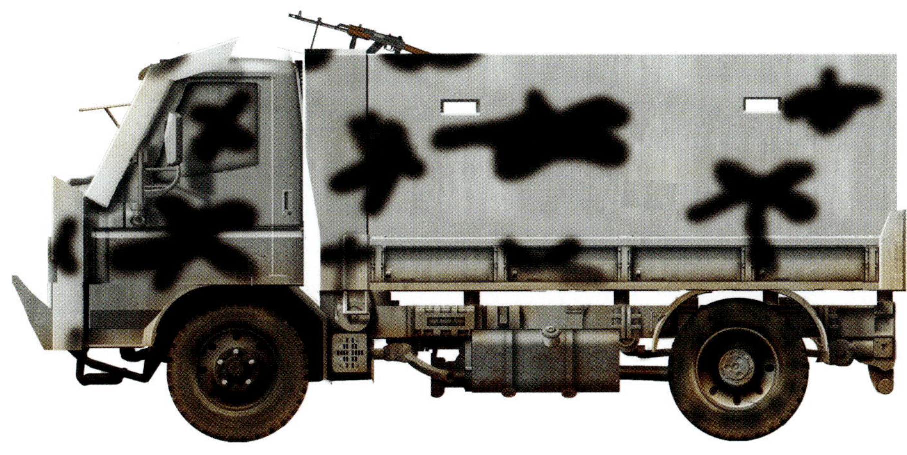

Another type of vehicle widely used by the Slavonic Corps were Hyundai and Iveco 3.5-ton trucks. Like the Chevrolets, they were fitted steel plates at the front and the top of their cabs, and were fitted with additional plates to protect the cargo hold. Most were over-sprayed overall in white, atop of which a disruptive camouflage pattern in black or dark brown was applied. None is known to have been armed, but passengers could use their personal weapons – including PKM and PKS machine guns – from within the vehicle. (Artwork by David Bocquelet)

In Syria during 2015, operatives of the Wagner Group arrived together with a number of UAZ Patriot SUVs. The majority of these were converted into 'technicals': civilian cars, SUVs or light trucks, armed with machine guns or light anti-aircraft guns, such as pintle-mounted PKM or PKS machine guns, or ZSU-23-2 twin 23mm guns. This example was equipped with a 14.5mm Dushka heavy machine gun, with a shield for the gunner. Most Patriot SUVs operated by Wagner PMC in Syria were also camouflaged – usually with whatever suitable colours were available. (Artwork by David Bocquelet)

Starting in 2017, Wagner PMC operatives deployed in Syria took over about 30 BRDM-2 armoured scout cars – and their variants – from stocks of the Syrian Arab Army. At least three variants (and numerous sub-variants) appeared in a matter of months, the first of which included the replacement of the original turret with a remotely-controlled ZU-23-2 23mm twin-barrel gun with large, box-like magazines on its sides. Additional ammunition was stored inside boxes distributed around the top of the vehicle. The front and sides of the hull were protected with slat armour to protect against the RPG threat. (Artwork by David Bocquelet)

The second most frequently seen BRDM-2 variant adapted by the Wagner Group saw the replacement of the original BPU-1 turret with a much taller construction mounting the 12.7mm NSV heavy machine gun and a 30mm AGS-17 automatic grenade launcher. Such vehicles were also protected by slat armour. Interestingly, unlike the first version shown, this version seems never to have been fitted with boxes for additional ammunition or other additional equipment. (Artwork by David Bocquelet)

The third version of the BRDM-2 developed by Wagner PMC from Syrian stocks was based on the chassis of disused 9P122 or 9P148 anti-tank guided missile carriers, and 9K31 Strela-1 SAM systems. Their primary weapons were removed, and the empty space thus created was protected by tall armour plates. Such vehicles were frequently fitted with PKM or PKS machine guns and a camera, as well as a canvas roof useful for protection of both a machine gunner and a forward artillery observer from the elements. Like the other two variants, such BRDM-2s also had slat armour on their front and sides. (Artwork by David Bocquelet)

One of very few vehicles of Russian origin operated by the Wagner Group in Syria was the BPM-97 Vystrel 4x4 mine-resistant ambush-protected (MRAP) vehicle. Developed since the late 1990s, this vehicle entered service in 2009–2013, and several were deployed during the Russian invasion of Ukraine in 2015. The BPM-97 is protected by welded steel armour able to withstand hits from 7.62 and 12.7mm weapons, and is usually not armed, although there is a version with a turret mounting machine guns of 12.7mm or 14.5mm calibre, or a pintle-mounted 7.62mm machine gun. (Artwork by David Bocquelet)

For operations in Libya, Sudan, and the CAR, operatives of the Wagner PMC were equipped with Chekan MRAPs. Based on the chassis of the Ural 4320 general purpose off-road 6x6 truck, and also known as 'Wagner Wagon', the Chekan is meant to serve as an infantry fighting vehicle with armour protecting against bullets and fragments. Checkans were further equipped with conical BPU-1 turrets (as used on the BTR-60PB APC and BRDM-2 reconnaissance vehicle) mounting a 14.5mm KPVT heavy machine gun with coaxial 7.62mm PKT machine gun as a secondary weapon. Behind it, the combat compartment has enough space for up to 10 infantrymen. (Artwork by David Bocquelet)

A simpler MRAP on the chassis of the Ural 4320 is the armoured personnel carrier variant known as Shchuka. This does not have a BPU-1 turret, but was custom-designed for transport of personnel, equipment and supplies. The hull roof has four upwards-hinging hatches, and two large doors at the rear, as well as a total of three ports on either side of the hull, enabling the passengers to fight from 'under armour', from within the combat compartment. While dozens of Shchukas and Chekans operated by PMCs remain in service in Syria and Africa, despite the addition of anti-mine trawls, their deployment in combat in Ukraine quickly demonstrated that they were much too vulnerable to the threat of mines, RPGs, and attack UAVs. Since 2023, many have been converted into trucks with armoured cabs. (Artwork by David Bocquelet)

In addition to Ural 4320 trucks, and the related Shchuka and Chekan MRAPs, in the CAR the Wagner Group also deployed numerous of so-called 'technicals': light trucks like this UNIMOG, armed with a pintle-mounted 14.5mm Dushka heavy machine gun. The majority of such vehicles had only makeshift camouflage (if at all), but this example and several Toyota SUVs belonging to one of Wagner's assault groups have a more elaborate camouflage pattern consisting of yellow sand overall, atop of which a disruptive camouflage pattern in thin stripes in black or dark olive green was applied. (Artwork by David Bocquelet)

During the Wagner Group's 'surge' in Libya in 2018–2020, the Russian mercenaries found themselves confronted with a particularly dangerous opponent in the form of Turkish attack UAVs like the Bayraktar TB.2. These are known to have destroyed several aircraft of the Free Libyan Air Force and dozens of technicals. To counter the Bayraktars, in early 2020 Wagner acquired about two dozen Pantsir S1 SHORADs from the UAE. Mounted on German MAN XS 45 8x8 trucks, and comprising a combination of two 2A38M 30mm automatic guns and 12 surface-to-air missiles, these were painted in sand overall, and expected to clear the sky of the Turkish UAVs. The idea did not work: the TB.2s destroyed up to 20 Pantsirs, and helped in the capture of several, together with their operators' manuals. (Artwork by David Bocquelet)

In summer 2017, the Wagner Group's operatives deployed to Syria were provided with a single BMPT-72 Terminator tank-support combat vehicle for testing purposes. Based on the chassis of an overhauled T-72 main battle tank, the BMPT was built to support tanks and other armoured fighting vehicles in urban combat. For this purpose, it was equipped with an array of optical devices and mounted four 9M120 Ataka-T ATGMs, two 2A42 30mm automatic guns (with 800 rounds), either two AG-17D or two AGS-30 30mm grenade launchers (with 600 rounds), and one PKTM 7.62mm machine gun (with 2,000 rounds). As far as is known, the vehicle saw some combat during the central Syria campaign of 2017 but was back in Russia by 2018. (Artwork by David Bocquelet)

Operatives of the Slavonic Corps deployed to Syria in October 2013 wore a variety of different uniforms, ranging from dark blue overalls of the Russian Ministry of Internal Affairs to whatever fatigues they were able to acquire online, in Russia, or in Lebanon. This mercenary – with a tattoo of the 'Rusich' symbol on his left forearm – is shown armed with an AK-103 7.62mm assault rifle. Usually issued to the GRU Spetsnaz, this example is fitted with shatterproof plastic parts – including the folding stock and pistol grip – and a red dot or similar optical sight. (Artwork by Giorgio Albertini)

Wagner PMC operatives in Syria were much better equipped than those of the Slavonic Corps. The majority wore the desert variant of the Gorka 3 Spetsnaz Uniform A, usually including a matching cap (Velcro adjustable), a jacket with reinforced elbows (with or without adjustable hood), trousers with loops for a wide belt and reinforced knees (tightened with elastic braid), body armour, a tactical vest with pouches for AK magazines, and hiking boots. Their principal firearm remained the AK-103, often an optical sight. (Artwork by Giorgio Albertini)

In addition to Russian nationals, in Syria, Mali, and the CAR, Wagner began hiring from the local population. This mercenary from the Central African Republic was equipped with a Spetsnas-style Kiver RSP helmet (with helmet cover) and a Bekas Atacs FG summer uniform (also worn by the Russian Coast Guard). Atop the latter, he has added an Operator-4 or BNZ plate carrier (with pouches for ammunition magazines), a medical pouch, X-form knee pads, and 6Sh 122 Ratnik gloves. His firearm is a 7.62mm AKM assault rifle. (Artwork by Giorgio Albertini)

About a dozen different Ilyushin Il-76 transport aircraft were used for moving Wagner operatives and arms around Africa, and especially to Libya, Mali and Sudan. One of the most interesting amongst them was the example with civilian registrations TL-KMZ and/or TL-KPA (both of which were seen at the same time in a video released by Prigozhin). This was frequently sighted at Bangui International between October and November 2021, in Benghazi in Libya and at Hmeimim AB in November and December 2022. Gauging from available videos and verbal reports, the jet was painted in white overall (except for the engine pylons, which are in matt black), had a light grey nose cone, and had no insignia except for the type designation under the cockpit and the small black registration on the rear fuselage. (Artwork by Tom Cooper)

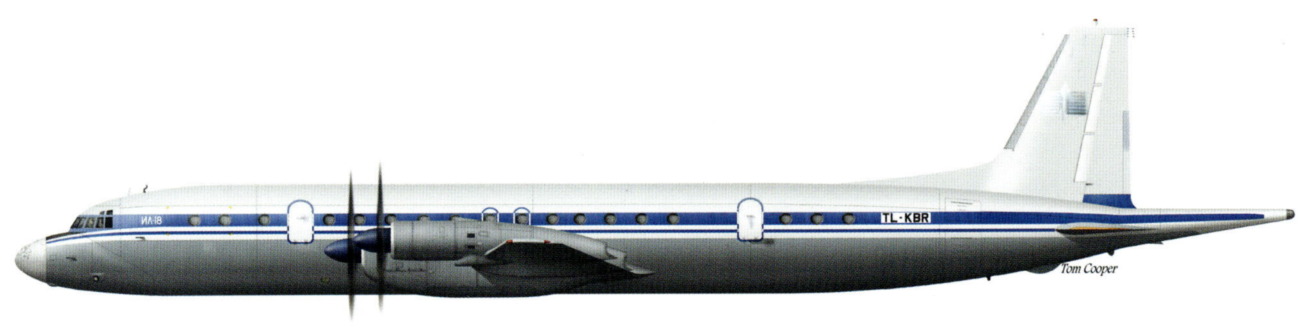


Another of the aircraft deployed intensively in the transport of Wagner operatives around Africa was this Ilyushin Il-18 (c/n 186009403) with the civilian registration TL-KBR. The aircraft originally served as a prototype for the Il-20 reconnaissance variant, with the registration RA-75713. After conversion to its 'transport configuration', it retained a 'sting' in the rear fuselage, carrying sensors for 'aerogeophysical research'. In early 2022, it was sighted multiple times in Libya (and at al-Jufrah AB), and then in Bahgui in February and March of the same year. This illustration shows it as seen in Bangui in October 2020. (Artwork by Tom Cooper)

Within the framework of Wagner PMC's involvement in Libya in early 2020, Moscow sold a total of 14 MiG-29 interceptors and Su-24M bombers to the Libyan National Army (LNA). On 18 May 2020, the first batch of six MiG-29s and five Su-24s was flown to Hmeimim AB, in Syria, under the guise of deliveries to that country. Actually, after having their Russian national insignia removed, and being used for fake photo sessions with Syrian personnel, on 24 May 2020 they were flown to Benina AB, outside Benghazi, in Libya. As of June of the same year, two Su-24s were photographed by satellites at al-Jufrah AB in central Libya, and four others at al-Khadim AB in the east of the country, leading to the conclusion that the total included six jets of this type. (Artwork by Tom Cooper)

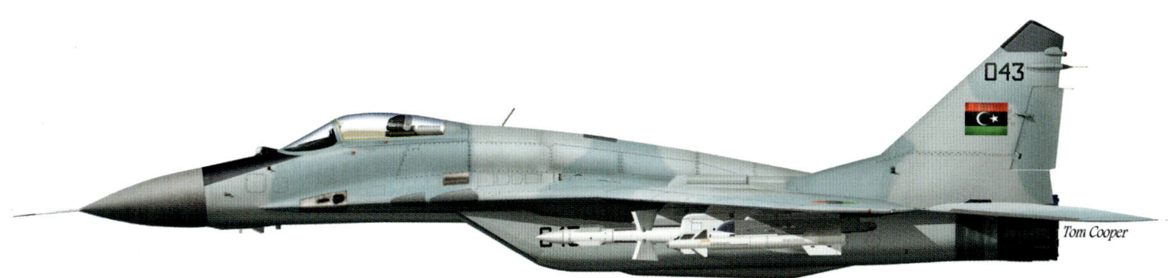


Just as the Su-24s delivered to the LNA were left in their typical grey and white livery, so also MiG-29s sold to Haftar's movement retained their colours applied while the aircraft were still operated by the Russian Aerospace Force. Although time and again shown surrounded by LNA personnel, according to releases by the US AFRICOM, for most of the following two years they were primarily maintained and flown by personnel provided by Wagner PMC. Both types had two- and/or three-digit 'bort' numbers, applied in black on intakes, repeated high on the fin. The MiG-29 '043' illustrated here is shown as armed with R-27R medium-range- and R-73 short-range air-to-air missiles. (Artwork by Tom Cooper)

In a clear demonstration of the close association of the Wagner Group with the GRU and thus the top Russian leadership, during their transfer from Hmeimim AB to Libya, Wagner-operated MiG-29s and Su-24s were always escorted by brand-new Su-35S fighter-bombers of the VKS. Amongst these was this example, bort number 21, which identified it as almost brand-new, delivered to the 790th Fighter Aviation Regiment of the VKS only in 2019. While escorting Wagner-operated MiGs and Sukhois from Syria to Libya, the jet was armed with four R-77-1, two R-27R, and two R-74 air-to-air missiles. (Artwork by Tom Cooper)

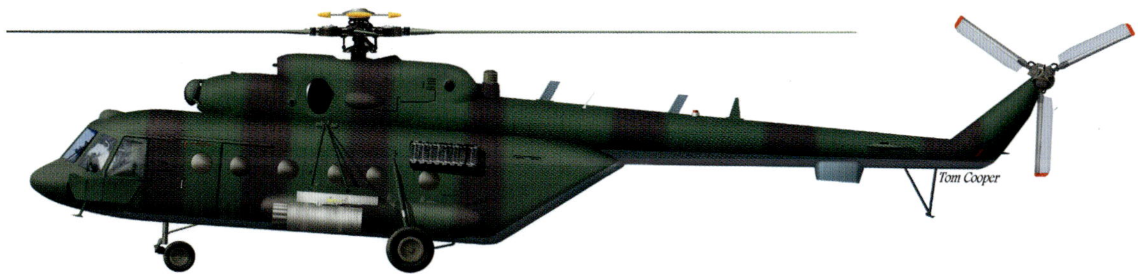


For the Wagner Group's adventure in Mozambique, the GRU prepared this Mi-8AMTSh assault helicopter: it was delivered to Nacala aboard a chartered Antonov An-124 transport aircraft in September 2019. Apparently in attempt to appear outwardly similar to the two Mi-8TVs operated by the Mozambiquan air force, it had a simple disruptive camouflage pattern in dark green and dark brown, with light admiralty grey on undersides – but wore no national markings or other insignia. The helicopter was armed with B-8M pods for 80mm unguided rockets, and carried a large chaff and flare dispenser on the rear sides of the cabin. (Artwork by Tom Cooper)

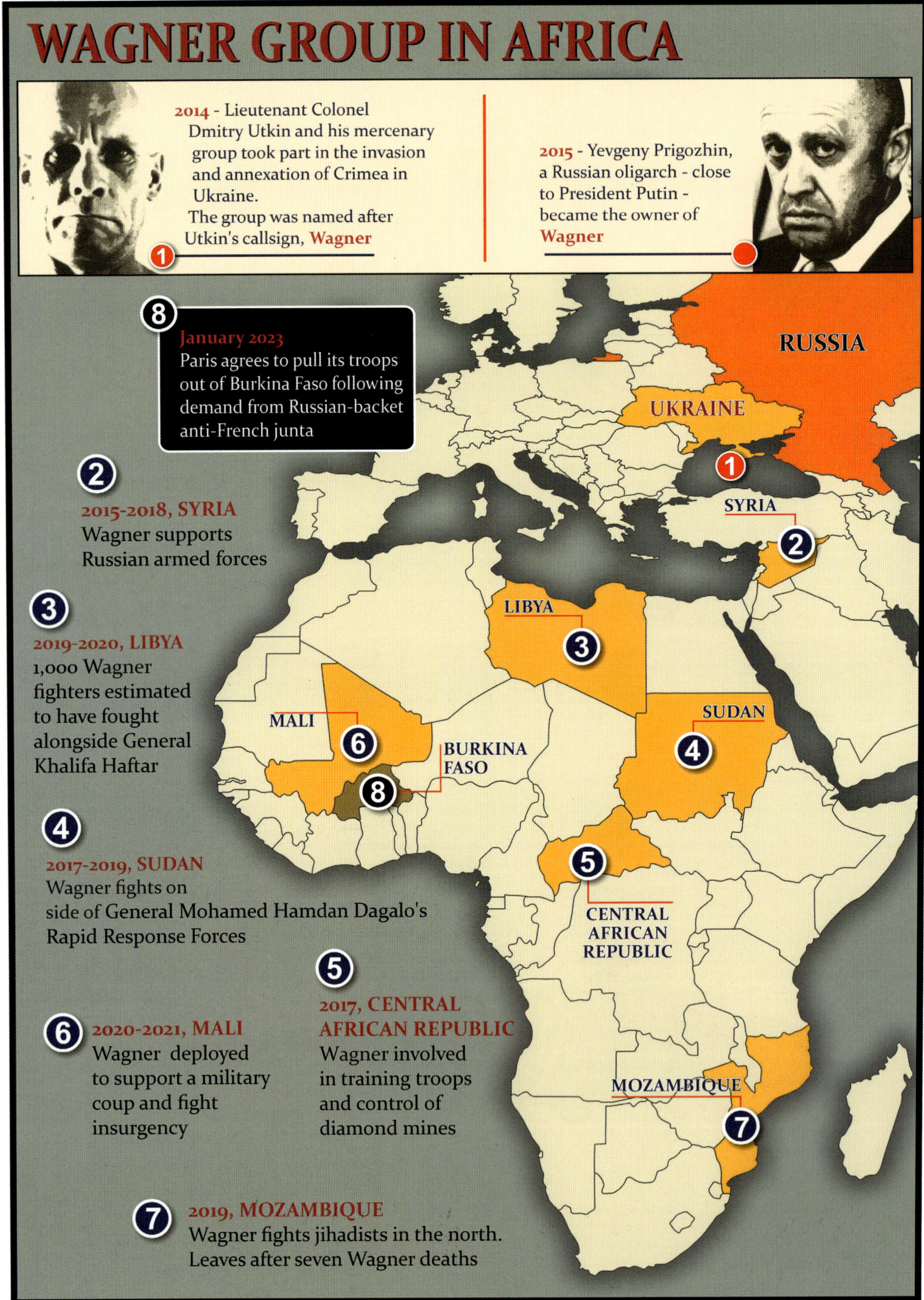


(Artwork by Anderson Subtil)

A BMPT-72 Terminator tank-support vehicle seen during its months-long deployment in Syria for testing purposes. As far as is known, starting from June 2017, the vehicle was operated by the Wagner Group. (Russian Ministry of Defence)

In conclusion, it is certain that the use of Wagner and other lesser-known Russian PMCs in Syria significantly reduced the losses of the Russian regular forces. It made the Kremlin capable of presenting its role in the country as an 'important success in the fight against terrorism' and to claim a 'major military victory', both at home and abroad.[31]

In February and March 2018, Wagner militants took part in additional battles around Damascus together with soldiers from the Russian special forces and soldiers of the Syrian government forces. At that time, the organisation had five company-sized units in Syria, including one called 'The Carpathians', consisting mainly of Ukrainians.[32]

After that, the number of Wagner operatives in Syria was reduced to 900 people.[33] They limited their activities to guarding and protection, consulting and training tasks, and only took part in minor operations. As a consequence, ever less was heard of them. However, they did remain in the country. In late 2019, when the US forces withdrew from parts of northern Syria, the American base in Manbij was occupied by Wagner operatives in cooperation with the nominally still US-supported SDF. Allied with Moscow since the 1980s, the leadership of the Turkish Kurd terrorist organisation was never too proud to welcome cooperation with its Russian allies.[34]

At the beginning of 2020, Wagner's men found themselves at odds with the Americans again, when US special forces blocked a convoy of mercenary vehicles in north-eastern Syria. Fortunately, there was no armed conflict in that case. The correspondent covering the case noted that the American forces remaining in Syria clashed with Wagner's men several times, but with no known casualties.[35] That it was not a unique event is clearly shown by the fact that several similar incidents took place between the American and Russian units serving in Syria, who mutually hindered each other's free movement.[36] On 25 August 2020, on one such occasion, a Russian and an American armoured personnel carrier collided, as a result of which seven American soldiers were slightly injured.[37]

In late 2020, Wagner mercenaries were deployed from Dayr az-Zawr province to Latakia, prompting ISIS to carry out more attacks against Assadist forces in the east of Syria.[38] In late 2021, the mercenaries launched a joint operation with regime forces, including several IRGC-controlled militias, against ISIS militants in Hama, Al-Raqqa and Dayr az-Zawr.[39] From the end of 2022, Wagner operatives took part in the fight against ISIS in central Syria,[40] while some of the personnel were redeployed to the Ukrainian front. However, even this was not enough, so the organisation started a large-scale recruitment campaign in Syria, from where several hundred mercenaries were recruited to fight in Ukraine.[41] It can be seen that although some of Wagner's militants had been withdrawn from Syria, the organisation was still in the country due to Russian interests.[42]

# 6
# MUSICIANS IN AFRICA

As far as is known the Wagner Group, sometimes referred to as 'musicians', appeared in Africa for the first time in 2017, when deploying about 2,000 operatives in Libya, and another 300 in Sudan.[1] Over the following six years, it widened its operations to a total of 24 African countries, with serious military activities in six of them: Burkina Faso, Central African Republic, Libya, Mali, Sudan, and Mozambique (until 2021). After the death of Prigozhin, from 20 November 2023 the Russian presence in the Sahel took the name 'Africa Corps' and General Adrey Averyanov was appointed as its commander.

## Purposes

In 2019 through the first Russia-Africa Summit in Sochi, the Kremlin accelerated its efforts to forge cooperation agreements with sub-Saharan African countries and since the invasion of Ukraine relationships in Africa have become even more important.

A Wagner document ranks African countries into three levels. The countries of the first level are Madagascar, Mali and the CAR, this level means that there is a great chance to influence the government according to Russian interests. In these countries, they planned to use a Syrian scenario, i.e. the goal was to obtain concessions in exchange for security services. The countries of the second level are Ghana (under President Nana Akufo-Addo) and Cameroon (under President Paul Biya). According to the document, these are the countries with which 'something can be done, but it is not yet clear what.' South Sudan (under President Salva Kiir Mayardit) belongs to the third group.[2] In addition to the Francophone sphere of interest, the Anglo-Saxon sphere of interest (i.e. Ghana and South Sudan) is also in Wagner's crosshairs. In the Democratic Republic of the Congo, Zimbabwe and Madagascar, there were only political strategists, often boosted by the presence of Russian 'bodyguards.' In Chad and Benin, Prigozhin's people worked with politicians close to the armed Muslim group Seleka. Prigozhin also had a special Africa team, 'Project Continent', of approximately 15 individuals with social media, political consultancy or information security backgrounds; 'These people all appeared to be taking instructions on ideological matters, countering media leaks and all military matters from "Mazay"', i.e. Konstantin Pikalov.[3]

The presence took place under various cover activities: military training/consulting, supervision of mining activities and in some cases, they played a kind of media role. In several places (e.g. CAR, Mali, and Burkina Faso) they pushed into the areas that were previously under French influence. In some countries, such as Algeria, Cameroon and Kenya, Wagner was only present for logistical purposes. These small deployments consisting of roughly 10 to 15 troops were tasked with facilitating arms transfers and training local personnel to use Russian-supplied equipment.[4] As of 30 September 2022, the Wagner Group was said to be temporarily no longer hiring mercenaries for African operations, but instead focusing on Ukraine.[5]

It is not known whether the African target countries were selected by Prigozhin himself or directly by the Kremlin, the only thing certain was that they coordinated.[6] It was highly likely, that once the Kremlin ordered a job to be done by the Wagner Group, the Russian state paid for it. If Prigozhin wanted to do his own business somewhere, he probably needed permission to perform military-type activities and it was his investment/burden. It was also likely, that the Russian state was against a sort of an 'overgrowth' of the Wagner Group's military activities around the world, since it means not only more costs, but more visibility and more risks as well.

From the beginning, Prigozhin opposed the presence of his mercenaries in the Ukrainian war, considering their activities much more useful in the African arena. Wagner's head in Africa was Colonel (retired) Konstantin Pikalov, alias Mazai (or Mazay) or 'The Colonel', or according to *Bellingcat* Wagner's 'Monsieur Afrique.'[7] Until at least 2007 he served as an officer of Russia's military unit 99795, located in the village of Storozhevo near St. Petersburg. Following retirement, he ran a private detective agency. After Pikalov made several trips to Republika Srpska in Bosnia and Herzegovina, Kazahstan, Finland, and Estonia – possibly to justify his freshly-issued Schengen visa (between 2015–2019, Pikalov received three Schengen visas issued by the Finnish consulate in St. Petersburg, all granted for 'tourism purposes') – he appeared in the Central African Republic and Madagascar. It is very likely that he also made stops in Sudan and Mozambique.[8]

The Colonel arrived in the CAR in early July 2018, approximately three weeks before the murder of three Russian journalists on 30 July (see below). He was initially assigned as campaign security chief to an early Russian favourite – Pastor Mailhol of Madagascar, and later to Andry Rajoelina, who went on to win the election. He returned to the CAR later in the summer of 2018.[9]

Pikalov was the only person in the CAR talking with Prigozhin without fear and as an equal, and his identity was not in fact known to Prigozhin's Africa-focused employees. He was careful to never be captured on camera without his sunglasses on, which made identification via facial recognition search impossible. He was finally identified through analysis of Valeriy Zakharov's phone calls. Two of the numbers he communicated with in 2019 belonged to a St. Petersburg-based company called Military Security Company 'Convoy'. The organisation had five individual shareholders, one of whom was also the CEO of Convoy; his name is Konstantin Aleksandrovich Pikalov, born on 23 July 1968. 'A search in reverse number-search apps showed that the numbers called by Zakharov and registered to Convoy were in fact used by Konstantin Pikalov.'[10]

## Adventures in Libya

In 2014 the Second Libyan Civil War erupted between numerous armed groups, primarily gravitating around the House of Representatives on one side, and the Government of National Accord on the other. Supported by Egypt and the UAE, The House of Representatives was headquartered in Tobruk, and its armed forces – the Libyan National Army (LNA) – controlled most of eastern and central Libya. Headquartered in Tripoli and Misurata (Misrata), the Government of National Accord (GNA) was recognised internationally as the official representative of Libya but supported by Turkey and Qatar only. Failing to control various well-armed militias and armed groups established during the revolution of 2012, it relied on support from powerful militias from Misurata to control parts of northern-central and western Libya. Moreover, in the wake of its unilateral decision to extend its mandate without elections, the GNA faced growing opposition in the east of the country. Indeed, in May 2014, the commander of the LNA, General Khalifa Haftar essentially staged a coup, established himself in control over eastern and central Libya, and then launched Operation Dignity – supposedly aiming to suppress the armed Islamist movements in Benghazi and Derna.

In reality, Haftar's LNA understood relatively little about the Islamists: indeed, it took years to 'defeat' them, mainly with use of extensive bribes, which convinced most of the organisations in question to side with the LNA. Indeed, thanks to support from Egypt, the UAE and later the Kingdom of Saudi Arabia, over the following months Haftar strengthened his position and managed to secure a number of major oilfields in the eastern part of the country. With the help of income from their exploitation, he became able to not only acquire ever-larger quantities of arms and ammunition from abroad but could also recruit mercenaries. In 2015, Moscow – probably emboldened by the UAE, and certainly attracted by the income from Libyan oil – decided to support Haftar's forces. By the end of the year, and in cooperation with the Moran Security Group and the RSB Group, Wagner operatives were in the country.[11]

The initial task of Wagner was the tactical training of LNA forces. At two bases in Libya, one in Benghazi and the other in Tobruk, it trained Haftar's troops to operate Russian-made weaponry, armoured vehicles, and artillery.[12] However, before long, the mercenaries were followed by operatives of the GRU and Spetsnaz. Moreover, via Cairo and Dubai, the GRU and Wagner established links with Sudan, where Haftar and the Russians began recruiting combatants of the Rapid Support Force (RSF). While the LNA thus eventually grew into a force up to three quarters of which consisted of defected Libyan Islamists and foreign mercenaries, Haftar became capable of planning and conducting major combat operations into central and western Libya.

In January 2017, Haftar met with Russian officials aboard the aircraft carrier *Admiral Kuznetsov* as it was on its way to Syria. The result was the agreement of Moscow to start providing support for the LNA. By then, the Russian mercenaries were not only helping with training and the construction of fortifications around major LNA positions, but also supporting operations of the Free Libyan Air Force through planning and guiding its air strikes and providing electronic warfare support.

Meanwhile, as the RSB Group was contracted to guard industrial facilities in the Benghazi area, the Wagner Group expanded its operations: while one group helped the LNA overhaul numerous T-55 and T-62 main battle tanks, and BMP-1 infantry fighting vehicles, another trained its snipers and yet another group trained the operators of newly-delivered 9M133 Kornet anti-tank guided missiles (ATGMs) (ASCC/NATO-reporting name AT-14 Spriggan) of Russian origin, in violation of a UN-imposed arms embargo. In turn Haftar granted Wagner control over al-Jufra Air Base and the Libyans and the Russians began planning an all-out attack on Tripoli by two assault groups including between 800 and 1,200 mercenaries. When this figure proved insufficient, the Russian PMC recruited between 1,500 and 1,600 Syrians to reinforce its forces in Libya.[13]

While the plaining for the coup in Tripoli was in full swing, and the aircraft of the Egyptian and UAE air forces flew clandestine air strikes on selected targets in western Libya, the LNA repeatedly clashed with forces loyal to the GNA. Early combat experience proved the Kornet ATGM to be highly effective. However, in turn the LNA began suffering heavy losses caused by Turkish-made unmanned aerial vehicles (UAVs), especially the notorious Bayraktar TB.2. Therefore, in 2018, Haftar (who had meanwhile promoted himself to the rank of field marshal) and the Russians agreed with the UAE to deliver about two dozen Pantsir S1 mobile short-range air defence systems (SHORAD) to be operated by the Russians. These were installed on the chassis of German MAN SX 45 8x8 trucks and consisted of a combination of two 30mm 2A38M automatic anti-aircraft guns and 12 read-to-launch surface-to-air missiles. These would provide crucial air defence for the advance of the two Wagner assault groups on Tripoli.[14]

In early April 2019, the LNA, led by two assault groups of the Wagner PMC, launched a surprise offensive from central Libya in the direction of Tripoli and Sirte in the north-west. Simultaneously, and largely overshadowed by developments around the capital, it advanced from Waddan on Sabha and Awbari in the south-west, until securing the local oilfields. Originally, this enterprise was planned to be conducted in coordination with a coup against the GNA in Tripoli, undertaken by a group of South African and Western mercenaries; however, this failed. Nevertheless, Wagner and the GNA quickly seized the towns of Gharyan and Tarhoun and then reached the outskirts of Tripoli and the international airport by advancing from multiple directions. Moreover, one of their columns turned west and secured the giant Woutya Air Base, together with dozens of combat aircraft and helicopters left from earlier times. However, the GNA resisted bitterly and supported by Turkey held out. By early 2020, in addition to Wagner operatives, both Ankara and Dubai had their forces deployed in Libya.

Ultimately, despite Emirati air strikes on bases used for Turkish shipments of arms and ammunition to the GNA, the TB.2 attack UAVs managed to suppress the Emirati-donated, Wagner-operated Pantsirs sufficiently for the government forces to start pushing the LNA ever further away from Tripoli. On their withdrawal, mercenaries of the Wagner Group left behind a huge number of mines and boobytraps: the position of many of these was disclosed when one of the Russians left behind a Samsung electronic tablet containing a related map.[15]

It was amid an imminent collapse of the GNA's year-long offensive into Tripoli and with Misuratan militias massing their troops for a counteroffensive against Sirte that in mid-May 2020 Moscow decided to sell a total of 14 old Mikoyan i Gurevich MiG-29 interceptors and Sukhoi Su-24M fighter-bombers to Haftar's LNA. These were delivered via Hmeimim AB in Syria, and home-based at al-Jufra and al-Khadim air bases. For at least the first six months of their operations in Libya, all were maintained and flown by Russian crews, recruited and provided by the Wagner Group.[16]

By July, militias allied with the GNA began massing for an attack on Sirte, and Cairo twice warned of its own military intervention in such an eventuality. In the light of growing tensions, and when it became clear that any further hostilities would lead to a major showdown including Turkey and Qatar on the side of the GNA, and Egypt, Russia, and the UAE on the side of Haftar's forces, in August 2020 Tripoli and Tobruk agreed to a UN-mediated ceasefire. Under the terms of this agreement all the foreign mercenaries were to leave the country.

This was entirely ignored by the Russians and as of 2021 Wagner PMC still had around 2,000 operatives in the country; and remained involved not only in providing training for the LNA but also in acts of intimidation of the population in the south of the country on behalf of Haftar. In late March 2022, about 1,300 Wagner mercenaries were withdrawn from Libya for deployment to Ukraine: still, around 900 remained, and their number then continued to grow until reaching between 1,500 and 2,000 in May 2022. Indeed, around the same time, the *Financial Times* put the total number of Russian private

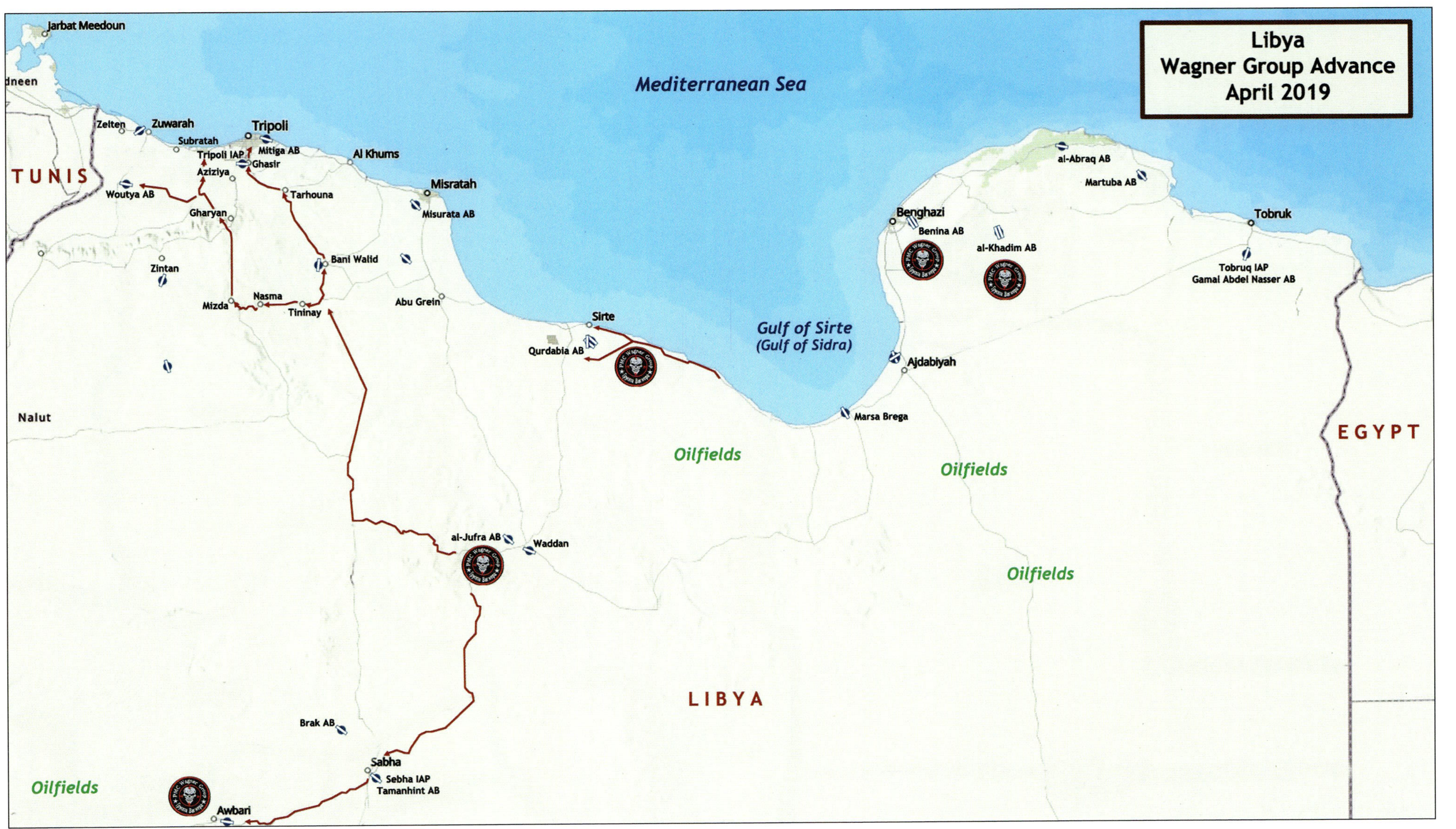


This map shows the Wagner-led LNA offensive in April 2019. Despite this offensive eventually managing to enter the outskirts of Tripoli and secure the international airport and Woutiya AB, ultimately, the forces involved proved insufficient for the task. This was to no small degree because both Haftar and Prigozhin were keen to secure the oilfields west of Awbari and Sabha, and thus sent a sizeable force in that direction. As a result, by March 2020, the GNA had not only recovered all of Tripoli and Woutiya AB but was on the verge of striking back at Sirte and Waddan and the local air bases. It was at that point in time that Moscow rushed MiG-29s, Su-24s, and other heavy weaponry to Libya, and threatened to launch a direct military intervention should the GNA continue its advance, thus freezing this conflict. (Map by Tom Cooper)

A destroyed Russian-made Ural 4320 truck, modified to serve as a 'gun truck', photographed after being abandoned by mercenaries of the Wagner Group. (Libyan Social Media)

A Chekan MRAP with Russian mercenaries seen withdrawing from Tripoli in May 2020. (Libyan Social Media)

A column of vehicles of the Wagner Group – including two Chekan MRAPs – underway in central Libya in May 2020. (Libyan Social Media)

Another part of the same column, showing a commercial 13.6-metre tilt-trailer carrying one of the Pantsir SHORAD systems donated by the UAE and operated by the Wagner Group. (Libyan Social Media)

military contractors in the country at 5,000, and a map revealed by one of Wagner's operatives indicated no fewer than 7,000.[17] Correspondingly, any kind of 'Russian withdrawal' from Libya was temporary at most, and it can be concluded that Moscow was determined to stick to its goals in this country.[18]

## With the Rapid Support Forces in Sudan

The military juntas in charge of Khartoum, the capital of Sudan, established close relations with Moscow during the presidency of dictator Omar al-Bashir back in the 2010. The presence of Russian military advisers – including helicopter and transport aircraft crews – can be traced back to around 2011. The cooperation intensified following a meeting between Putin and Bashir in Sochi in November 2017, when the Sudanese agreed to let the Russians construct an air base outside Port Sudan.[19]

The first presence of the Wagner Group can be traced back to 2017, when around 300 operatives were deployed in the country with the task of training combatants of the notorious Rapid Support Forces (RSF), led by Mohammed 'Hemetti' Hamdan Dagalo. Their services – and some of the Russian weaponry delivered – were partially paid for by the UAE and partially through concessions for several gold mines controlled by the RSF, arranged via Meroe Gold. This subsidiary of Prigozhin's M Invest Group appeared in Sudan together with Wagner's mercenaries in the form of geologists and construction workers, accompanied by construction materials, mining machines, lots of specialised- and military vehicles, and two Mil Mi-8 helicopters.[20] In turn, during anti-regime protests in Khartoum in 2019, Meroe Gold imported 13 tons of riot control equipment including police shields, helmets, and rubber batons.

After being subjected to sanctions by the USA, Meroe Gold was renamed al-Solag Mining and remained an important supplier of Esnaad Engineering, owned by Hemetti's family. As of 2020, the Wagner operations in Sudan were directed by Alexandr 'Ratibor' Sergeevich Kuznetsov: this veteran mercenary had served as the commander of the 1st Attack and Reconnaissance Company since 2014 and was redeployed to Sudan after suffering a combat injury while fighting with the LNA in Libya in 2019.[21]

In cooperation with the Sudanese Defence Forces and the national Intelligence and Security Services, the extracted gold was then smuggled out of the county using Russian and Sudanese military aircraft via Khartoum International. Once brought to Dubai, the gold was re-exported all over the world and used not only to buoy the Kremlin's gold reserves necessary to lessen the impact of Western sanctions imposed following the invasion of Ukraine in 2014, but also to finance Wagner's operations in Sudan and in the CAR. Moreover, in February 2022, when Putin launched the full-scale invasion of Ukraine, Hemetti arrived in Moscow with US $30 million worth of gold and additional mining concessions.[22]

## The Episode in Madagascar

'Mazai' Pikolov of Wagner PMC arrived in Madagascar in 2018. He was first tasked with supporting Russian protégé André Mailhol, and then, with his weakening, he supported Andry Rajoelina in the presidential election, which the latter then won. Support for the candidate was also directly facilitated by three citizens of the Russian Federation: Andrey Kramar, Roman Pozdnyakov and Vladimir Boyaritsev. Reportedly, all three came from St. Petersburg, and acted on behalf of Prigozhin.[23]

> "Wagner failure here was rooted in its struggle to understand of local context and its overall lack of political experience.", because "the PMC analysts lacked sufficient background knowledge about Madagascar, and some had no prior experience conducting political field work. These operatives eventually supported the victor, Andry Rajoelina, in the later rounds of the election—more through process of elimination than strategy."[24]

According to the statement of the former director of Kraoma Mining, the Madagascan state company Kraomita Malagasy (which was established as the successor of the chrome mining company COMINA), cooperated with the Ferrum Mining company, which was a shell company managed by Prigozhin: allegedly, this was how the Wagner Group was rewarded for its support during the elections of 2018.[25]

Wagner`s mining operations met with worker strikes and public opposition. However, the PMC learned a lot from the developments and drew the appropriate conclusions: first, it developed extremely intensive propaganda activity, aiming to influence public opinion. Unsurprisingly, a news platform was set up to push propaganda and it is near-certain that this effort was supported from revitalisation projects in Toamasina. As is known from the US Senate's resolution issued in February 2021, the Malagasy government officially denied (and continues denying) the presence of the Wagner Group.[26]

In January 2022, Tana and Moscow signed an agreement for military cooperation, which included a plan for the provision of equipment and training. Ever since, Russia has supported Madagascar's claim to the Éparse Islands, including Bassas da India, Europa, Glorieuses, Juan de Nova and Tromelin. Uninhabited, and with a total area of 53.2 square kilometres, these remain under French jurisdiction. Relations with the French were further soured by the fact that the head of state's former Malagasy-French adviser and a former French colonel were imprisoned in 2021 on charges of preparing an assassination attempt against the president. In early October 2022, the foreign minister of Madagascar was acquitted because he voted in the UN against sanctions due to Russia's aggression in Ukraine.

On 19 January 2023, on behalf of the Malagasy government, Foreign Minister General Rakotonirina Léon Richard continued to deny that the Wagner Group was present in his country.[27] It cannot

One of up to eight MiG-29s delivered by Russia to Haftar's forces in May 2020 photographed at an air base in Libya. Although wearing the national markings of the FLAF, the jet was initially operated by Russian pilots serving with the Wagner Group. (Libyan Social Media, via Arnaud Delallande)

During their transfer to Libya, MiG-29s and Su-24Ms sold to Haftar and some of the transport aircraft hauling other arms and equipment to Libya (in violation of the UN arms embargo) were regularly escorted by Su-35S interceptors of the Russian Aeropace Force forward deployed at Hmeimim AB. This Su-35S was photographed from a Boeing P-8A Poseidon of the US Navy over the Mediterranean Sea during one such operation on 28 May 2020. (US Navy)

be ruled out with absolute certainty that part or all of Wagner's staff may have been withdrawn from the island due to the war in Ukraine.

On 16 November 2023, a presidential election was held again on the island and Rajoelina was re-elected. On 17 August, just six days before his death, Mamy Ravatomanga – a Malagasy businessman and the head of the Sodiat group – met Prigozhin during an African tour to discuss the organisation of Andry Rajoelina's personal security. In June the French nationality of the president became a major political scandal. A coalition of 11 candidates called for the exclusion of Rajoelina from the presidential election. Prigozhin was in Africa in August 2023 after Wagner PMC stopped participating in the Russian-Ukrainian war and had attempted to organise a military coup in Russia. During the meeting Ravatomanga expressed doubts about Rajoelina's ability to win and the discussions focused on the acquisition of personal security services to ensure the safety of the President and his property in all circumstances. Prigozhin agreed to send at least 300 soldiers at a cost of $15,000 per month for each fighter, i.e. $4.5 million per month.[28]

## Failure in Mozambique

In 2018, a contingent of 160–300 people (according to other sources 200 people arrived in September 2019, and according to the

A convoy of SUVs belonging to the Wagner Group is seen here entering the CAR from Sudan, led by a Chekan MRAP. (Doklad-Razvedki)

group's own records, their number rose to 2,000 people) arrived in Mozambique to help fight against Al Shabab jihadists, estimated at 1,500–4,000 people settled in the northern part of the country, who posed a threat to the Cabo Delgado gas fields, where even the interests of the French company Total were threatened.[29] In exchange Wagner received access to the country's liquified natural gas reserves and other natural resources, including diamonds. In view of the rich gas fields, the international community was very willing to help (France, the USA, and even the EU promised trainers).[30]

Fighting alongside the 12,000-strong Mozambican army, Wagner was given a base at Nacala in August 2019. President Filipe Nyusi and Putin signed a bilateral defence agreement. On 13 September 2019 an Antonov An-124 delivered 160 guns-for-hire and a few days later another Antonov delivered a Mi-17 helicopter to the Wagner Group in Nacala.[31] Wagner PMC received additional reinforcements in March 2020 by Antonov An-124 and by train. From April 2020, Umbria Aviation, a South African PMC equipped with Gazelle helicopters (deployed since 2013), and the Dyck Advisory Group led by Lionel Dyck from Zimbabwe, also joined them.[32]

Nevertheless, the Wagner Group left the country in May 2020 because it suffered very serious losses. Part of the reason for the defeat was the very difficult terrain consisting of extensive dense forest, which provided an excellent hiding place for the jihadists. A further contribution to the defeat was that the Wagner fighters were basically unable to communicate with the local forces due to language difficulties and mutual distrust.[33] The Russian technical staff, on the other hand, remained at the Nacal base, and a listening station was established.

It seems that the Russians wanted to eliminate the Wagner Group at all costs, and increased their local presence. Rosneft produced gas with Exxon Mobil based on concessions in the Zambezi Delta and the Angoche basin. The Russian diamond giant Alrosa was also able to conduct research in Mozambique.[34] It should be noted that Prigozhin strongly supported Nyusi's presidential election campaign mainly through the famous Onda da Frelimo Facebook account and the AFRIC Group, the latter led by Jose Matemulane, a Mozambican living in St. Petersburg.

## Victory in the Central African Republic

Complete chaos ensued in the Central African Republic after the withdrawal of the French Operation Sangaris on 31 October 2016. The county had been under a UN arms embargo since 2013 and in 2018 government forces only controlled 20 percent of the country's territory. They turned to Russia for help, who officially sent trainers under the UN mandate, but Wagner had unofficially infiltrated the system.[35] A Wagner contingent of 450 people also arrived here in January 2018, after the United Nations granted Russia a waiver to send trainers, weapons, and equipment to Bangui in December 2017. Within the framework of a Russian-CAR interstate treaty, they received mining concessions in exchange for military assistance.[36]

Wagner were directly involved in fighting against rebels and breaking up anti-government demonstrations. The CAR became the main operational field of Wagner PMC in Africa with about 2,000 mercenaries deployed there in 2022. The Russians set up their command and training base at the former imperial residence of Berengo.[37]

Training was carried out at the military base in Berengo (75km from Bangui) and presumably at the base in Sibout. One source stated there were at least 175 trainers, while another stated 500 trainers.[38] They also carried a significant stockpile of weapons, which coincided with the lifting of the UN arms embargo. According to sources in the CAR, part of the Wagner Group has become a quasi-praetorian guard for President Faustin-Archange Touadéra, and they have assisted in arresting and torturing the opposition. Others have helped with communication, training or other FACA (Armed Forces of CAR) activities.[39]

In 2018, three Russian journalists came to the CAR from the Investigation Control Centre supported by Mikhail Khodorkovsky, Orkhan Dzhemal, Aleksandr Rastorguyev, and Kirill Radchenko to find out what exactly the PMC was doing there, but they were murdered. A letter from Mazai testifies to an order for their surveillance.[40] The story of what happened is worth examining in more detail because it reveals Wagner's relationship system, operational structure and fundamental mistakes in the CAR.[41]

On 30 July, 23km from the town of Sibut, the journalists were stopped and shot by unknown persons, their bodies were found three metres from their car and the driver, who was also their

Another Checkan MRAP (note the UBM-1 turret atop the superstructure) with a group of Russian mercenaries after arriving in the CAR from Sudan. (CAR Social Media)

interpreter, fled. On 31 July, the news appeared on Facebook that the three journalists had been murdered at a checkpoint in CAR. From London, Khodorkovsky funded an investigative team to find out what happened. First, they found the fleeing driver and he told what happened. According to the driver's version, an Arabic-speaking group in turbans stopped the car, attacked them, and confiscated all their belongings. However, the truth of the version told by the driver, according to which Wagner was not involved, was quickly challenged. Meanwhile, the colleagues of the murdered journalists also questioned President Putin himself at a press conference. Putin's answer was that he regretted what had happened and then noted that the journalists made a mistake because they had not informed the local authorities about their trip, and that they arrived not as journalists but as tourists. According to him, they were killed by local group members, the case was being investigated and the result would be received through diplomatic channels. Three years later there was still no result.[42]

Meanwhile, Khodorkovsky's group, *Dossier Center*, sent professional investigators to the scene and offered money in exchange for information. The driver's version soon proved false: the investigators obtained the telephone data of the journalists' driver and analysed his calls. It turned out that he only used that phone when the Russian journalists arrived at the CAR and he was in constant contact with a certain Emannuel Kotofio, a gendarme in the CAR trained by the Russians. Kotofio's cell phone data was also obtained and it turned out that he had been shadowing the journalists all along, staying close to them as soon as they entered the territory of the CAR. It was also revealed that Kotofio was in contact with Alexander Sotoff, Prigozhin's spy chief in the Wagner Group. Sotoff's cell phone information was also obtained, and it was revealed that he was in close contact with Valery Zakharov, former head of Wagner in the CAR and one of the president's closest official advisers during the period under investigation.[43]

Several witnesses talked about the fact that before the execution of the journalists, another car also drove by, and Kotofio was also identified with three other white people among the passengers of the car. It turned out that everything was planned in advance and the Russians had been lured into a trap. *Dossier Centre* made a 3D model of the execution scene and it turned out that the perpetrators were professional snipers. Despite the heavy rain the snipers shot with high precision. Each body received six or seven targeted shots, which eliminated the theory of a robbery, in addition to which the killers did not take anything, and the journalists' money was only stolen later at the commissariat. Beside the vital organs, Kirill was also shot in the leg. His head and neck were injured as if someone wanted to strangle him and he was tortured before the execution.

The Wagner PMC acquired interests in the local diamond mines via Diamville and Lobaye Invest, and gradually became involved in logging at Bois Rouge, and they were also present in the export of sugar and coffee and supervised the transit traffic between Bangui, in CAR, and Douala, a seaport in Cameroon.[44] Wagner manages its interests in the CAR through Wagner subsidiary companies, Lobaye Invest, SEWA Security Services and OUIS (Officer's Union for International Security) to provide a veneer of legitimacy:

- SEWA provides protection for senior CAR government officials and has also claimed to provide 'instructors' for 'training exercises' in the CAR. In January 2023 the company was being designated under the US Government's Executive Order 13667.
- OUIS: The Wagner Group started to use this front company based in Russia for its operations in the CAR since early 2021 and claims to represent Russian 'instructors' in CAR. The director of OUIS is Aleksandr Aleksandrovich Ivanov who served as the National Security Advisor to CAR's President. OUIS was also being designated under E.O. 13667.
- The Wagner Group uses aircraft provided by Kratol Aviation to move personnel and equipment between the CAR, Libya, and Mali. Kratol was being designated under E.O. 13667 for having materially assisted, sponsored, or provided financial,

A mercenary of the Wagner Group, accompanying a number of local combatants: over time, the Russians began recruiting and training the latter. (CAR Social Media)

material, logistical, or technological support for, or goods or services.[45]

- JSC Aviacon Zitotrans (Aviacon Zitotrans) is a Russian cargo airline that shipped defence materiel to Venezuela, Africa, and other locations. Zitotrans has an interest in four Russia-registered Ilyushin aircraft with tail numbers RA-76842, RA-76502, RA-76846, and RA-78765.

These companies were connected to Prigozhin`s Concord group and characterised by regularly changing their owner, director, name and headquarters in what has been described as 'a permanent game of chess.'[46]

The Wagner Group became active mainly in December 2020, in the 'recapture' of the country, after the armed forces of the former president, Bozizé, set out in 2020 to overthrow Touadéra's presidency and by January 2021 they had already brought two thirds of the country under their control.[47] Valery Sakharov, the president's security policy adviser, was also a member of the group and requested and received instructions directly from Mazai.[48] According to Wagner's own database, about 10,000 of their members were in the territory of the CAR in 2022, its largest contingent in the territory of one country in Africa, and had 13 military bases in 2023.[49]

From the second half of 2021, Wagner carried out more and more operations completely independent of FACA, while also taking a role in FACA training. According to surveys, while 27 percent of the operations were carried out with FACA, 70 percent of their independent operations were against civilian targets.[50] Wagner's tactic was not to clash with the insurgent groups, but rather to take control of civilians in the areas controlled by the insurgent groups and, according to analyses, essentially carry out a number of self-serving, opportunistic operations. At the same time, Wagner played a kind of supervisory role over FACA.[51]

The first evidence of Wagner's atrocities in Africa was a *zachistka* on 2 June 2021 near to Bocaranga, on the common CAR-Chad border, filmed by a surveillance plane of a neighbouring state. Ten days beforehand, 10 Wagner mercenaries had been killed near that location. A *Zachistka* (зачистка) is a clearing operation as conducted by the regular Russian army in Chechnya, in which everyone must be eliminated and no (potential) enemy can be left behind. The aerial video shows a Wagner convoy stopping and its members getting into a conflict with two local people, one of whom is shot dead in the bush.

Separately, several women testified to documentary filmmakers that they had been raped by Wagner mercenaries. Suzanne, a mother of four children, for example testified that they went to sell fruit at a Wagner military base. There, she was forced into a building and raped by several people. A CAR soldier then escorted her home and the soldier said he could not do anything as the Russians were their bosses.[52]

According to a 2021 UN Human Rights report, FARC and Wagner mercenaries were responsible for 491 victims in 240 cases, with 144 civilian deaths verified. One of the cruellest cases was the murder, burning, and dismemberment of a Muslim merchant in Kaga Bandoro on 6 May 2021. The house of one of the richest merchants in the town was looted. Since almost no traces were left, it was impossible to prove that, according to eyewitnesses, the perpetrators were Russians.[53]

According to UN report AL CAF 2/2021,[54] on several occasions Wagner`s mercenaries committed torture in the CAR, especially during interrogation detentions, including waterboarding, electric shocks, sleep deprivation, limb amputation, sexual violations as a weapon of war, including sexual violations against boys and men. The seriousness of certain crimes makes them a war crime and a crime against humanity. The Russians deny committing these crimes and have not sanctioned the perpetrators. In July 2021 the execution of a dozen people in Bossangoa was attributed to Wagner.[55]

Ten years after the coup of March 2013 in which Seleka rebels triggered a civil war, on 21 January 2023 in the north-west, Coalition of Patriots for Change (CPC) rebels launched a new offensive against government forces and targeted the Béloko customs post in Nana-Mambéré prefecture. Béloko is CAR's first customs checkpoint on the trade corridor between Bangui and Douala in Cameroon, and the main source of its customs revenue. The second attack on 25 January took place in Gordil, in north-eastern Vakaga prefecture, and the third on 14 February in Sikikedé, the confrontation claimed over a dozen lives from both sides, including seven Wagner combatants, 'The group's growing presence in Vakaga is linked to the ministry of mines' September 2022 decision to forbid local prospectors from working gold production sites in Vakaga and neighbouring Bamingui-Bangoran, in order to allow Russian mercenaries to operate the mines.'[56]

In May 2023, residents of the KM5 neighbourhood of Bangui closed their businesses and protested against ongoing violence by mercenaries. According to residents, the Wagner Group`s fighters pursued, kidnaped, raped and tortured several Central Africans. The protest was preceded by a series of kidnappings of local residents: mercenaries captured Mr Chekh Samdjida Mahamat Chibeké, his relative, whose name was Harun, and 70-year-old Mahamat Amat Hafid Moussa Bachir. After several hours of torture, the 'Wagnerites' freed two of them. Chibeké, according to local publication *CNC*, was admitted to hospital and fell into a coma. The fate of the elderly Bachir remains unknown.

Chibeké was first taken to Camp De Roux, where he was placed in a small cell before being transported to Bazoubangui hill located just behind the camp. The Wagner mercenaries began beating him on his loins and feet, causing the victim unbearable pain. When a leader arrived on the scene, he ordered the abuse to stop without giving the victim an explanation.[57] The rage of the people increased and the president's official adviser from Wagner, former member of the French Foreign Legion Vitali Perfilev, was forced to offer the weak explanation that the mercenaries would cooperate with the police or with gendarmerie. Perfilev was working for Valeri Nikolayevich Zakharov former chief of Wagner in the CAR, and became an official adviser to Touadéra, just like Zakharov before him, and 'While Zakharov has gradually distanced himself from Bangui, Perfilev has risen in rank, becoming the right-hand man for the CAR of Dmitri Utkin.' In December 2020, when the country's CPC armed groups went on the offensive, he was the main military commander charged with defending Bangui and then the Russian-Central African counterattack aimed at opening up the capital.[58]

The head of the Wagner Group's 'civilian' branch in the CAR is Dmitry Syty. In 2018, he participated in the discussions that led to the Central African Peace Agreement signed in Khartoum in February 2019 and subsequently broken off at the end of 2020. Targeted by a letter bomb on 16 December 2022, he was evacuated to Russia for medical reasons.[59] In May 2023 he returned to Bangui. After the death of Prigozhin Syty was rumoured to be the group's new frontman.

On 26 and 27 January 2023, Wagner mercenaries supported by FACA soldiers carried out violent attacks for several hours against the positions of the rebels of the CPC 11km from Gordile, then at Ndomboloye on the Mossabio axis. During this operation, Wagner deployed all its military power in the country, including its helicopters and its military aircraft. After its first patrol in the vicinity of the capital Bangui, Wagner`s L-39 Albatros aircraft carried out its first aerial bombardments during the attack. According to local sources, the plane did not do much, no missile was fired, and it was reported that 'they feel like this plane is dropping lemons on them.' The main purpose of its deployment appeared to be a demonstration to the president of CAR that Wagner was now also deploying an air force.[60]

Ndassima, the largest gold mine of the CAR, is worth 2.5 billion euros. From 2010, it belonged to the Canadian company ASMIN, however in December 2018 the CAR government gave the concession to Midas Resources, based in Madagascar. Later, a call for tenders for Passendero field was announced on 15 Nov 2019, that had previously belonged to a company called Aurafrique. Midas is connected to Kraomita Malagasy SA, a company that bought military equipment, weapons, shields and helmets, for the company Lobaye Invest, registered in CAR and which may have been connected to Prigozhin. M Finance is the third affiliated company with the same address as the parent company of Prigozhin: Concord Catering. All these front companies cover businesses based on a 'nesting doll' network, like the classic post-Soviet company system.[61]

Wagner's activity in the country was not viewed as purely negative, as some neutral press in the CAR reported. On 16 April 2023, a vehicle driven by a priest and carrying eight people struck an explosive device near the town of Niem-Yéléwa. Russian COSI instructors being nearby provided first aid to the victims and evacuated them to hospital.[62] In early July, several foreign sources claimed that an unknown number of Wagner mercenaries were leaving the Central African Republic, information firmly denied by the government. According to a statement by COSI, led by Alexander Ivanov,[63] in mid-July 2023 several hundred Wagner fighters arrived in the Central African Republic to provide security 'in anticipation of the referendum of 30 July 2023.'[64]

Prigozhin's revolt of 23–25 June 2023, has had consequences for Wagner's deployment in Africa: relations between the 1,600 Russian mercenaries and the junta in Mali have deteriorated at least in part because of Bamako's payment difficulties. In contrast, in the CAR, where the group was financing its intervention through mining licenses, relations remained stable as of 2023.[65]

From March to May 2024, Wagner trained the Azande Ani Kpi Gbe (AAKG) militia in Obo. For nearly two years, the Haut-Mbomou prefecture had been the scene of incessant violence. The bloody clashes between the AAKG militiamen and the rebels of the UPC (Unit for Peace in the Central African Republic) have left behind a trail of destruction and desolation, causing many victims among both the fighters and the civilian population. After nearly two months of training a hundred AAKG militiamen joined the ranks of FACA.[66]

## Victory in Mali

Wagner appeared in Mali with about 500 people as a result of the coup on 24 May 2021.[67] Since then, according to Russian sources, their number has risen to 3,000. With the help of the local civil initiative called Yerewolo, a very effective pro-Russian campaign was carried out, with the aim of replacing the mainly French peacekeepers (Operation Barkhane and Task Force Takuba) with Russians, more specifically with the Wagner Group.[68] According to a 2021 survey, 81 percent of the population were opposed to Barkhane, and 87 percent were in favour of the Wagner Group (which had just arrived at the time).

CAR troops, trained by Wagner, prepare for their next mission. (CAR Social Media)

Wagner-trained troops of the Central African Army with their 'Technical'. (CAR Social Media)

In 2013, only 20 percent of the territory of Mali was at risk of terrorism, in 2022 this was 90 percent, and the military junta was waiting for the securing of its position by the Russians. Colonel Sadio Camara, Minister of Defence since June 2021, became the liaison to the Russian group.[69] The Russian PMC sent 500 people to Bamako in December 2021 under the leadership of Ivan Maslov (being in his 40s, he had also been present in Ukraine, Iraq, and the CAR) and built a logistics base here. Later another 500 people were sent to the country. They brought with them one Mi-35 helicopter and one Su-25 Frogfoot aircraft to provide air support (the latter crashed in October 2021) and five Aero L-39C Albatros training jets deployed as ground attack aircraft. The main difference compared to their presence in the CAR was that in the CAR they demonstrated strength and patrolled from the beginning, while in Mali they initially tried to hide until the Bamako base was fully developed in order to make their presence as discreet as possible.[70]

On 15 August 2022, after Task Force Takuba, Operation Barkhane also left Mali. The bases at Menaka and Gao were taken over by the Wagner Group after that, and joint patrols with the Malian Armed Forces (*Forces Armées Maliennes*/FAMa) began. In contrast to the CAR, it is understood that independent Wagner operations were not yet carried out there.[71] These were said to have become so effective that the Islamist group GSIM (*Groupe de soutien à l'islam et aux musulmans*, also known as JNIM) and the regional drug dealers were forced to move their area of operation further north.[72]

In Gao, tension arose between the Wagner Group and the German contingent of MINUSMA (United Nations Multidimensional Integrated Stabilization Mission in Mali), because the base was used by both sides and they were forced into cooperation, which the Westerners did not like. Because of this situation the British planned to withdraw their troops from MINUSMA in 2023 and the Germans by May 2024.

According to an investigation in November 2022, the Wagner Group (in addition to FAMa) was also allegedly involved in the deaths of 370 civilians, as well as in sexual crimes and crimes against humanity, and they participated in looting of the population and the driving away of their animals.

Wagner also engaged in disinformation activities, which in one case went badly. An accusation was made that before the French withdrawal under Operation Barkhane, that six people arrested at Gossi were killed by the French, and this information was spread through social media. But the French, for precaution's sake, had left a drone near the Gossi base after the evacuation, which Wagner did not know about. The drone monitored how Dongfeng pick-ups, used by Wagner, arrived 12 hours after the French evacuation, and later how six victims were buried by members of the Wagner Group four kilometres from the base. The people who made recordings published on the internet for Wagner also added fake subtitles seen on the recordings. Wagner's propagandists made the fatal mistake of forgetting to erase from the video recording the conversation in Bambara amongst their Malian partners: they talked about strongly disputing the version told by the Russians that the mass grave was left behind by the French. The French leaked the classified drone recording and managed to identify the person on VK (Russian Facebook) who created the fake news.[73]

More serious cases were the Dogofry and Mourai massacres in central Mali on 27 March 2022, in which Wagner's participation is disputed. The Human Right's Watch version, similar to that of GSIM, claims that Mi-24s and 35s used by the FAMa and the Wagner Group, and a Eurocopter Super Puma, machine-gunned the market on Sunday at noon. GSIM itself admits that there were 30 jihadists in the city. According to FAMa's version, about 200 jihadists were killed after about 30 jihadists from the crowd fired at the helicopters beforehand.[74]

The Wagner Group has also tried to acquire its own resources in Mali. Individuals connected to the group obtained concessions in the area of gold mines through the companies Alpha Development and Marko Mining at the end of 2021 and in April 2022.

According to news from 17 March 2023, Wagner's forces in Bamako also have SA-22 Pantsir self-propelled air defence systems. According to 2023 data, Wagner's presence costs the country $10 million (6 billion CFA francs) per year. From this it is estimated that 1,000–1,400 mercenaries are paid a monthly salary of approximately 7,000–9,000 euros.[75] By way of comparison, the Ministry of Justice of Mali has a budget of half this amount, and the Ministry of Health has twice this amount of budget, and thus it represents a very significant financial burden for the country.

The Wagner media campaign in Mali is led by Maxim Shugaley, a self-taught sociologist without a degree and the president of the National Heritage Protection Foundation. According to his own authority, he has been examining the Malian society for several decades and has stated that Operation Barkhane was not fighting terrorists but was supporting them.

Wagner's media campaign has prepared false witness statements with a local people.[76] For example, in one of their videos, a person introduces himself as a member of the Malian Islamist movement Katibat Macina, saying that the French supported an attack against FAMa bases. In the second step, an African newspaper belonging to Prigozhin's Patriot media group published this video in an article with a shocking headline 'France supports terrorist groups.' Here we note that the Patriot Group includes more than 224 media partners, TVs, websites and the news agency RIA FAN (РИА ФАН). In the third phase, other websites belonging to the group also announced the fake news, with similarly shocking headlines. In the fourth step, the news agency RIA FAN takes the news material.[77] Although they have made very basic errors, for example, in one of their news stories the uniform of a 'French' officer was clearly marked 'US Army', it seems that they have managed the emotions of the population more skilfully; they do not conflate the Islamic religion with terrorism, jihadists and Tuaregs, as, for example, French media and French politicians very often do.[78]

According to French reports, Wagner's business model in Mali is characterised by self-financing and 'pilot fish behaviour'. Their activity is similar to that of drug dealers: at first, they provide security services for free, and the invoice is presented only later. In Mali, the monthly fee is US $10 million for the deployment of 1,200 people. Faced with the payment difficulties of its Malian client until the lifting of ECOWAS sanctions against the country in July 2022, the Russian private military company arrived at a lasting and lucrative solution; in July 2022 three gold mines in southern Mali came under Wagner's control after the mining laws were changed directly in favour of Wagner PMC.

The Russian mercenaries set up two mining companies and have since been trying to obtain mining permits with the support of Malian businessmen. Their interest in gold has increased tenfold since the start of the war in Ukraine. Prigozhin's men also embarked on artisanal gold panning, investing in at least three sites south of Bamako, and in gold trafficking via Dubai, the hub of its illegal trade.[79]

Wagner commissioned two Russian geologists, Viktor Popov and Sergei Laktionov, to bring their mining activities to fruition on the banks of the Niger River. The latter had participated in the group's first surveys in the country between July and December 2021. After having created a first mining company under Malian law, *Alpha Development*, at the end of 2021 through a local nominee, the two men founded a second, *Marko Mining*, in April 2022. At the same time, Sergei Laktionov had several meetings with officials, including Colonel Adama Bakayoko, a close friend of General Alou Boï Diarra, Chief of Staff of the Air Force. A linchpin of the deployment of Wagner, the latter acts in the shadow of the Russophile Minister of Defence, Sadio Camara. To the Malian authorities, Laktionov asked to review the exploitation permits of three prolific gold mines for the benefit of Wagner:

- Fekola, currently exploited by the Canadian mining company B2Gold;
- Loulo-Gounkoto, whose permit is held by another Canadian mining company Barrick Gold,
- and finally, Syama, awarded to the Australian company Resolute Mining.

The first two are located in the southwest of the country, near the border with Senegal, and the third in the southeast, near Ivory Coast. In June 2022, Lamine Seydou Traoré, Minister of Mines and brother-in-law of Sadio Camara, visited Russia, officially to participate in an economic forum in St. Petersburg.[80] Another important project has also attracted the attention of the Wagner Group: Mali could become the first lithium producer in West Africa, where in Goulamina, about 150km from Bamako, Australian mining company Firefinch Limited and the Chinese company Ganfeng Lithium will make their joint project a reality.[81]

An ambush at Tinzaouten on 27 July 2024 reportedly killed 84 ex-Wagner fighters and 47 Malian soldiers. Several reports suggested that Ukrainian special forces had trained and provided necessary reconnaissance and intelligence information for Tuareg rebels in Mali against the Russian PMC.[82]

## Overlooked Effort: Burkina Faso

In Burkina Faso, the Wagner Group probably appeared in 2018 when Russia-Guinea signed an intergovernmental military cooperation agreement. The Russian PMC was allowed to guard Russia's investments in Guinea.[83] After that, very little was heard about the organisation. Two coups took place in the country in 2022. Prigozhin personally welcomed the coup d'état on 23–24 January, and his aim was to gain ground here, but Paul-Henri Sandaogo Damiba, who came to power, opposed Wagner's intention in this direction and remained a supporter of the French federation. The Wagner Group then sided with Ibrahim Traoré and helped him

A still from a video released by Prigozhin, showing the cockpit of one of the Il-76 transports deployed in support of the Wagner Group's operations in Africa. Clearly visible are stickers with two fake civilian registrations: TL-KPA and TL-KMZ, both worn by the same aircraft frequently sighted in the CAR and Mali of 2021–2022 (for additional details, see the colour section). The stickers served as 'reminders' for the crew, and the registrations were applied and removed, or re-applied as necessary. (Wagner Group)

overthrow Damiba on 30 September 2022. As in Mali, Wagner – or other Russian groups closely related to Wagner – performed a disinformation campaign and other similar activities hiding behind social media and local civic bodies. They were able to show very remarkable results, especially in terms of winning hearts and minds of the young population (cf. the influence of Western media on the Arab Spring; it should also be noted that in this area, the Western-French activity in relation to the population appeared to be dramatically weak).[84] Wagner helped the anti-French campaign, actively distributed posters, produced a multitude of small videos and animations, and even produced video games for the local youth showing the French as zombie colonisers, in which of course the forces of Wagner rush to the aid of the locals.[85] Community agitation was launched against Damiba using fake profiles, and in relation to the extent of the intervention, it is appropriate to refer to Russian activity in the American presidential election campaign. It is therefore no wonder that the crowd protesting during Damiba's departure chanted anti-French slogans and waved Russian flags.

On 27 March 2023, journalists of the French newspapers *Libération* and *Le Monde* made public a video received in February showing the torture of seven children and adults at a military base in northern Burkina (Ouahigouya). Even before the announcement the propaganda department of the Wagner Group, or a propaganda agency close to the group, started a campaign to discredit the French journalists, accusing them of receiving tens of thousands of euros in exchange for discrediting the Burkinabe army and the transitional government.[86] As the military junta announced the loss of control over 40 percent of the country and would enlist every man and woman over the age of 18 to fight against terrorist groups, a wiretap of an Ivorian counter-terrorism officer was leaked to the media, according to which Wagner, and Russian foreign policy, was preparing the destabilisation of Ivory Coast, relying on Wagner's presence in Mali and Burkina Faso.[87] There was also information that the Russian PMC had already established its foothold in neighbouring Niger and started building its relations with the new military junta leaders.[88]

In mid-April 2023, the Traoré junta resumed its relationship with the European Union that had been severed in September 2022, and prior to that, American PMCs also appeared near the Burkinabe army. In 2019, the annual military Exercise Flintlock took place in Burkina Faso and Mauritania, with the participation of about 2,000 commandos and 32 African countries, with the aim of training special units to fight against AQMI (Al-Qaeda in the Lands of the Islamic Maghreb).[89]

In Loumbila, about 20km northeast of Ouagadougou, the Russians installed the first military base of their newly labelled Africa Corps in December 2023.

## Across the Big Pound: Venezuela

Russia has also gained significant influence in Venezuela in South America, in the 'backyard' of the USA. Venezuela has a socialist system, alongside Cuba and Nicaragua, and although it has significant mineral wealth, is one of the poorest countries on the South American continent.[90] The current president, Nicolás Maduro, owes much of his power to Cuban, Turkish, Russian and Chinese financial support.

One of the most reliable allies of the current regime is Russia, which has established close diplomatic, political, financial, economic and military cooperation with Venezuela. Russian companies such as Gazprom, Rosneft, TNK-BP, Surgutneftgaz, and Lukoil have a significant stake/influence in the Venezuelan oil industry. Today, the country's biggest creditor and investor is Russia, for which the country is important not only for the protection of its investments, but also from a strategic point of view, especially because of its proximity to the USA, which is considered its primary opponent. This is probably due to the fact that Russia also plays a significant role in the preparation, training and arming of the Venezuelan military with, for example, Su-30MK2s fighter jets and S-300 surface-to-air missile systems, and which also provides a smaller military contingent including consultants and trainers, stationed in the country.[91]

More and more Venezuelans however have had enough of impoverishment, deprivation, soaring inflation, various economic and other restrictions, and therefore in 2017, anti-regime demonstrations began in the country, which lasted until the 2018 parliamentary elections. The opposition presidential candidate Juan Guaido, who has the support of the USA and the EU, came very close to gaining power. On 23 January 2019, Guaido announced that he had won the election, but the military and administration did not support him, and Maduro declared that he considered himself the winner of the election. A stalemate developed that could have even led to a civil war. It was vital for Russia that its trusted ally remained in power. However, in addition to political and financial support, this also required some more tangible support on the ground. This was the Wagner Group, which had a significant part in the fact that the change of power did not materialise.

The Wagner Group arrived in the country in 2018, with up to 400 personnel in two waves, to support President Maduro.[92] The PMC and their equipment was transported by Russian AN-124 and IL-76 transport aircraft.[93] The Russian PSC was given multiple tasks, including defence of government buildings and critical infrastructure, especially oil installations used by Rostneft.[94] In addition, together with Cuban agents, they were also involved in the protection of President Maduro.[95] In 2018, Wagner's men also took part in the training of members of the Venezuelan National Militia and the pro-Maduro *Colectivos* paramilitaries, thereby actually influencing the elections, as members of the Maduro-funded *Colectivos* often acted violently against opposition activists and broke up their events.[96]

Part of Wagner's job was to find and hunt down foreign anti-government fighters in Venezuela, which resulted in the elimination of many of them. As a result of a failed armed coup attempt in May 2020 even two former US soldiers were captured.[97] With these services, Wagner was able to ensure that Maduro could retain his power and that Russian interests in the country would not be undermined.[98]

In exchange for the Wagner Group's services, the Russians were given the opportunity to exploit the raw materials (oil, gas, iron, aluminium, gold and even diamonds) in the Orinoco Basin. Not only the Russians, but also the Chinese and Iranians are interested in the mineral called Thorium, found in Venezuela, which has similar properties to Uranium, but without radioactive waste as a byproduct of its processing and use. According to some sources, the Russians have already acquired a stake in the mines, which are protected by the Wagner Group. It has also been suggested that Russia could station a small military contingent in the country. Wagner's armed forces have also taken part in a military exercise in Venezuela held near the Brazilian border.[99]

According to some sources, Wagner has 1,000 employees in Venezuela.[100] American secret materials leaked in 2023 indicate that the Wagner Group is present not only in Venezuela, but also in Haiti, and fearing the growth of its influence, the American leadership planned countermeasures.[101]

According to some experts, the Wagner Group has also set foot in Sri Lanka, but their activities have been kept secret until now.[102] This is likely to be related to the training of the Sri Lankan army and other armed forces, as Russia has significant military, security and intelligence cooperation with Sri Lanka.[103] According to the investigative portal *Molfar Global* and other sources, in addition to the Wagner Group, the Russian PMC organisations RSB Group,[104] Moran,[105] Vega Strategic Services/Vegacy Strategic Services,[106] and Ferax (Feraks) also have interests in the country.[107] The Russian state-owned Emercom Demining and RusCorp carry out mine clearance and guarding tasks in the country in cooperation with Gazprom and Transneft.[108] Russian PMCs operate relatively freely in the country, thanks to the fact that it is extremely indebted and faces serious economic difficulties, for the solution of which they asked and received help from the country's old ally and supporter, Russia, as well as China, India and Japan.[109]

# SOURCES / BIBLIOGRAPHY

Specific sources refereed to in the writing of this work are cited in the individual endnotes. The full bibliography and wider list of sources can be downloaded from our website https://www.helion.co.uk/public-downloads.php

# NOTES

## Chapter 1

1 Ehl, 'More than mercenaries'; Joseph Siegle, 'How Russia is pursuing state capture in Africa', *LSE*, March 21, 2022, https://blogs.lse.ac.uk/africaatlse/2022/03/21/how-russia-is-pursuing-state-capture-in-africa-ukraine-wagner-group/, accessed: 9 January 2023.

2 Dossier Center`s document, https://dossier.center See 'Wagner, les mercenaires de la Russie (2/2)', Benoit Bringer, Forbidden Films – ARTE France – Mediawan Rights, 2023.

3 'Putin Chef's Kisses of Death: Russia's Shadow Army's State-Run Structure Exposed', *Bellingcat*, 14 August 2020, https://www.bellingcat.com/news/uk-and-europe/2020/08/14/pmc-structure-exposed/ accessed: 21 July 2023.

4 Catrina Doxsee, 'Putin's Proxies: Examining Russia's Use of Private Military Companies', *CSIS*, September 15, 2022, https://www.csis.org/analysis/putins-proxies-examining-russias-use-private-military-companies, accessed: 9 January 2023.

5 Philippe Randrianarimanana, 'Le groupe Wagner ne recrute plus pour l'Afrique, guerre en Ukraine oblige', *TV5 Monde*, 10 October 2022, https://information.tv5monde.com/afrique/le-groupe-wagner-ne-recrute-plus-pour-l-afrique-guerre-en-ukraine-oblige-474133, accessed: 9 January 2023.

6 Sergey Sukhankin, 'The 'Hybrid' Role of Russian Mercenaries, PMCs and Irregulars in Moscow's Scramble for Africa', *The Jamestown Foundation*, 10 January 2020, https://jamestown.org/program/the-hybrid-role-of-russian-mercenaries-pmcs-and-irregulars-in-moscows-scramble-for-africa/, accessed: 9 January 2023.

7 Or 'wagnerians.' For the various nicknames of the group see 'Sotrudnikov 'CHVK Vagnera' ne stesnyayutsya pokazyvat' po TV', Wagnera, 17 February 2021, https://wagnera.ru/smi/sotrudnikov-chvk-vagnera-ne-stesnyayutsya-pokazyvat-po-tv, accessed: January 9, 2023.

8 'Qui est Konstantin Pikalov, soupçonné d'être le 'Monsieur Afrique' du groupe paramilitaire Wagner?', *RFI*, 19 August 2020,nhttps://www.rfi.fr/fr/afrique/20200818-konstantin-pikalov-le-monsieur-afrique-wagner, accessed: 20 March 2023.

9 'Putin Chef's Kisses of Death: Russia's Shadow Army's State-Run Structure Exposed', *Bellingcat*, 14 August 2020. https://www.bellingcat.com/news/uk-and-europe/2020/08/14/pmc-structure-exposed/, accessed: 20 March 2023.

10 'Putin Chef's Kisses of Death: Russia's Shadow Army's State-Run Structure Exposed', *Bellingcat*, 14 August 2020. https://www.bellingcat.com/news/uk-and-europe/2020/08/14/pmc-structure-exposed/, accessed: 20 March 2023.

11 Marshall Guzansky, 'Outsourcing warfare'.

12 Sergey Sukhankin, 'Continuation of Policy by Other Means: Russian Private Military Contractors in the Libyan Civil War', *Terrorism Monitor* 18, no. 3, February 7, 2020.

13 Courtin, 'The transfer of Russian arms', Samuel Ramani, *Russia in Africa: Resurgent Great Power or Bellicose Pretender?* (Hurst Publishers, 2023), pp. 210–211.

14 Courtin, p. 214.; Jones et al., 'Russia's Corporate Soldiers', p. 43; Joseph S. Bermudez Jr., Brian Katz, 'Moscow's Next Front: Russia's Expanding Military Footprint in Libya', *Center for Strategic and International Studies*, June 17, 2020, https://www.csis.org/analysis/moscows-next-front-russias-expanding-military-footprint-libya

15 Ramani, *Russia in Africa*, pp. 256–262, 304.

16 'Russia, Wagner Group complicating Libyan ceasefire efforts', US AFRICOM, July 15, 2020, https://www.africom.mil/pressrelease/33008/russia-wagner-group-complicating-libyan-cease

17 Ramani, *Russia in Africa*, p. 305; Heinemann-Grüder, Aris, *Russian Analytical Digest*, 3; 'Russia reduces number of Syrian and Wagner troops in Libya', *Financial Times*, April 27, 2022, https://www.ft.com/content/88ab3d20-8a10-4ae2-a4c5-122acd6a8067, accessed: 20 March 2023; The presence of Wagner PMC in Africa (2022) See Wagner`s recruitment sites: www.join-wagner.com and www.wagnera.ru.

18 Emile Bouiver, 'Les sociétés militaires privées russes au Moyen-Orient (2/2). En Libye, le groupe Wagner à la manœuvre', *Les clés du Moyen-Orient*, November 18, 2022, https://www.lesclesdumoyenorient.com/Les-societes-militaires-privees-russes-au-Moyen-Orient-2-2-En-Libye-le-groupe.html#nh57, accessed: 9 January 2023.

19 András István Türke, 'La compexité de la crise du Darfour', *CERPESC 08/AF/03/2008*, March 2, 2008, https://www.academia.edu/3426793/Soudan_La_complexit%C3%A9_de_la_crise_du_Darfour.; János Besenyő, *Darfur Peacekeepers - The African Union Peacekeeping Mission in Darfur (AMIS) from the Perspective of a Hungarian Military Advisor* (Paris: L'Harmattan, 2021), p. 40, p. 96. Notably, Port Sudan is a port city on the Red Sea and the place where the country's oil-pipelines end.

20 Sukhankin, 'The 'Hybrid' Role of Russian Mercenaries', Aris Heinemann-Grüder, *Russian Analytical Digest*, 3. The RSF is the successor to the Janjaweed Sudanese Arab militia group. See Türke, 'La compexité de la crise du Darfour', *CERPESC 08/AF/03/2008*, March 2, 2008, https://www.academia.edu/3426793/Soudan_La_complexit%C3%A9_de_la_crise_du_Darfour, pp. 8–9; Philip van Niekerk,

'Analyse. Comment le Groupe Wagner tisse sa toile en Afrique', *Courrier International*, March 15, 2023, https://www.courrierinternational.com/article/analyse-comment-le-groupe-wagner-tisse-sa-toile-en-afrique., accessed: 20 March 2023; Jason Blazakis, Colin P. Clarke, Naureen Chowdhury Fink, Sean Steinbeg, 'Wagner Group: The Evolution of a Private Army (Special Report)', *The Soufan Center*, June 2023, 19; Oscar Rickett, 'Le groupe Wagner ' s'enrichit au Soudan ' grâce aux mines d'or et au gouvernement, Une enquête du New York Times met en lumière les concessions minières soudanaises du groupe de mercenaires russes', *Middle East Eye*, June 9, 2022, https://www.middleeasteye.net/fr/actu-et-enquetes/soudan-russie-groupe-wagner-mine-or-gouvernement-massacres, accessed: 9 January 2023.

21 Blazakis et al., p. 12.

22 Ramani, *Russia in Africa*, pp. 219–223, 273–281, 306–307; Marten, p. 17; Nedele, 'The Long Arm(s) of the State', pp. 14–17.; Sutanuka Sinha Ray, Laxmipriya Das, 'Intervention of Russian Private Military Forces in the Conflicts of 21st Century', *International Journal of Law Management & Humanities* 4, no. 4 (2021), 734, https://doij.org/10.10000/IJLMH.111323, accessed: 9 January 2023.

23 Marc Nexon, 'Moscou à la manœuvre à Madagascar, Un documentaire de la BBC raconte comment la Russie a financé les campagnes de plusieurs candidats à l'élection présidentielle à Madagascar en décembre 2018', *Le Point*, April, 17, 2019, https://www.lepoint.fr/monde/moscou-a-la-manoeuvre-a-madagascar-17-04-2019-2308315_24.php, accessed: 9 January 2023.; Ramani, *Russia in Africa*, pp. 224–227.

24 Catrina Doxsee, 'Putin's Proxies: Examining Russia's Use of Private Military Companies', *CSIS*, September 15, 2022, https://www.csis.org/analysis/putins-proxies-examining-russias-use-private-military-companies, accessed: 9 January 2023.

25 'Gros plan sur les organigrammes des sociétés contrôlées par le groupe russe Wagner en Afrique (Rapport)', *Ecofin Pro*, February 23, 2023, https://www.agenceecofin.com/mines/2302-105809-gros-plan-sur-les-organigrammes-des-societes-controlees-par-le-groupe-russe-wagner-en-afrique-rapport, accessed: 9 January 2023; Jones et al., 'Russia's Corporate Soldiers', pp. 58–59.

26 *RESOLUTION Expressing the sense of the Senate that the activities of Russian national Yevgeniy Prigozhin and his affiliated entities pose a threat to the national interests and national security of the United States and allies and partners of the United States around the world.* February 3, 2021, https://www.coons.senate.gov/imo/media/doc/TEXT%20Prigozhin%20resolution%201-2021.pdf.

27 'Mpikarama an'ady 'Wagner': mila mailo hatrany i Madagasikara, Manamafy ny tsy fisian'ny mpikarama an'ady rosianina 'Wagner', ny minisitry ny Raharaham-bahiny mpisolo toerana, ny Jeneraly Rakotonirina Léon Richard, omaly. 'Mila mailo hatrany anefa i Madagasikara', hoy izy', *TanikoMadagascar*, 19 January 2023, https://tanikomadagascar.wordpress.com/2023/01/19/mpikarama-anady-wagner-mila-mailo-hatrany-i-madagasikara/, accessed: 20 March 2023.

28 Vincent Masikati, 'Rajoelina addressed PMC Wagner before the elections to protect his power in Madagascar', *Harare.com*, 5 November 2023, https://iharare.com/rajoelina-addressed-pmc-wagner-before-the-elections-to-protect-his-power-in-madagascar/

29 Jones et al., 'Russia's Corporate Soldiers', p. 60.; Petersohn, 'The anti-mercenary norm', p. 111.

30 However, even Eric Prince's Blackwater failed like Wagner. The French finally managed to send Rwandan 'mercenaries' to the region instead of French units, at the beginning of July 2021, with European Union funding. They became one of the best-equipped African armies and were stylishly called 'the Wagner of France' or 'the Wagner of the EU.' See Norman Ishimwe, 'L'armée rwandaise est-elle en train de devenir le Wagner de la France et de l'Europe?', *Jambonews*, 14 February 2022, https://www.jambonews.net/actualites/20220214-larmee-rwandaise-est-elle-en-train-de-devenir-le-wagner-de-la-france-et-de-leurope/, accessed: 9 January 2023; EUTM-MOZ (Since 3 November 2021.) See 'About European Union Training Mission in Mozambique', *EEAS website*, 12 September 2022. https://www.eeas.europa.eu/eutm-mozambique/about-european-union-training-mission-mozambique_en?s=4411, accessed: 20 March 2023.

31 Ramani, *Russia in Africa*, pp. 228–230.; Jones et al., 'Russia's Corporate Soldiers', p. 60.

32 Dyck Advisory Group's base was 180km from the conflict zone, it was not effective because it could not solve the fuel supply problems for the Gazelles and it lacked the means to enable deployments in the north. See Achraf Tijani, 'Mozambique: face aux jihadistes, les troupes de la SADC peuvent-elles pallier l'échec de l'armée? Les chefs d'État de la Communauté de développement d'Afrique australe (SADC) ont décidé d'intervenir militairement dans le pays. Cependant, ce soutien extérieur risque de ne pas suffire', *Jeuneafrique*, 7 July 2021, https://www.jeuneafrique.com/1198528/politique/mozambique-face-aux-jihadistes-les-troupes-de-la-sadc-peuvent-elles-pallier-lechec-de-larmee/, accessed: 9 January 2023.

33 Ramani, *Russia in Africa*, p. 230; Sebastian Elischer, 'Populist civil society, the Wagner Group and postcoup politics in Mali', *West African Papers, OECD Publishing*, no. 36 (2022), p. 24.; Sukhankin, 'Russian Mercenaries Pour Into…'.

34 'Malgré le départ de Wagner, Moscou reste impliquée au Cabo Delgado', *Africa Intelligence*, 12 February 2021, https://www.africaintelligence.fr/afrique-australe-et-iles/2021/12/02/malgre-le-depart-de-wagner-moscou-reste-impliquee-au-cabo-delgado,109708351-gra, accessed: 9 January 2023.

35 Interview with Jean-Serge Bokassa, Minister of the Interior of the CAR (2016–2018) in *Wagner, les hommes de l`ombre de Poutine* (documentary).

36 Benjamin Sami Hemche, *Overt Partnership, Covert Intervention Russian use of mercenaries in the Central African Republic* (Master's Thesis, Swedish Defence University, 2021).

37 Olivier Mathieu, 'Centrafrique-Russie: qui est Vitali Perfilev, le patron de Wagner à Bangui ?', *Jeuneafrique*, 1 April 2022. https://www.jeuneafrique.com/1334939/politique/centrafrique-russie-qui-est-vitali-perfilev-le-patron-de-wagner-a-bangui/, accessed: 9 January 2023.

38 Sukhankin, 'The 'Hybrid' Role of Russian Mercenaries',; Heinemann-Grüder, Aris, *Russian Analytical Digest*, 3.

39 Marten, p. 17.; Jones et al., 'Russia's Corporate Soldiers', pp. 54–58.

40 Ramani, *Russia in Africa*, pp. 202–206.

41 Summary, based on the Final Report on the Murder of Orkhan Dzhemal, Aleksandr Rastogruev and Kirill Radchenko in the Central African Republic, *Dossier Center*, https://dossier.center/car-en/, accessed: 15 July 2023.

42 Wagner, les mercenaires de la Russie (2/2), Benoit Bringer, Forbidden Fims - ARTE France – Mediawan Rights, 2023

43 Apparently, the driver made the fundamental mistake of using the same SIM card to communicate with the Russian journalists and the contact person of the Wagner spy network, thus greatly facilitating the investigations. For the authors' part, we also express our doubts about the fact that the Khodorkovsky team bought this information only for money, without the help or (technical) intervention of the intelligence services of other Western countries. (AIT)

44 'Pendant la guerre en Ukraine, le Groupe Wagner tisse sa toile en Afrique', *Radio France*, 4 March 2023, https://www.radiofrance.fr/franceculture/podcasts/les-cartes-en-mouvement/pendant-la-guerre-en-ukraine-le-groupe-wagner-tisse-sa-toile-en-afrique-5595005, accessed: 20 March 2023; 'CAR: Prigozhin's Blood Diamonds', *AEOW*, December, 2022, https://alleyesonwagner.org/2022/12/02/car-prigozhins-blood-diamonds/.

45 'Treasury Sanctions Russian Proxy Wagner Group as a Transnational Criminal Organization', US Department of the Treasury.

46 Wagner, les mercenaires de la Russie (2/2)

47 Ramani, *Russia in Africa*, pp. 267–272.

48 Tancréde Chambraud, 'Qui est Konstantin Pikalov, soupçonné d'être le 'Monsieur Afrique' du groupe paramilitaire Wagner?', *RFI*, August 18, 2020, https://www.rfi.fr/fr/afrique/20200818-konstantin-pikalov-le-monsieur-afrique-wagner, accessed: 9 January 2023.

49 Bénédicte Tassart, 'Afrique: l›influence de la milice Wagner de plus en plus visible, Le groupe de mercenaires Wagner est déjà implanté dans 24 pays africains. Le conseiller à la sécurité du président centrafricain est membre de cette milice', *RTL*, 28 February 2023, https://www.rtl.fr/actu/international/afrique-l-influence-de-la-milice-wagner-de-plus-en-plus-visible-7900240001, accessed: 20 March 2023.

50 'Les opérations du groupe Wagner en Afrique, les tendances du ciblage de populations civiles en République centrafricaine et au Mali', *ACLED*, 30 August 2022, https://acleddata.com/2022/08/30/les-operations-du-groupe-wagner-en-afrique-les-tendances-du-ciblage-de-populations-civiles-en-republique-centrafricaine-et-au-mali/, accessed: 9 January 2023

51 Ramani, *Russia in Africa,* pp. 308–310; Nedele, 'The Long Arm(s) of the State', pp. 23–25.

52 Wagner, les hommes de l`ombre de Poutine (documentary).

53 RAPPORT PUBLIC SUR LES VIOLATIONS DES DROITS DE L'HOMME ET DU DROIT INTERNATIONAL HUMANITAIRE EN REPUBLIQUE CENTRAFRICAINE DURANT LA PERIODE ELECTORALE, Juillet 2020 – Juin 2021, MINUSCA – UN Human Rights, Office of the High Commissioner, 2021., p. 5. and p. 18.

54 Mandats du Groupe de travail sur la question de l`utilisation des mercenaires comme moyen de violer les droits de l`homme et d`empêcher l`exercice du droit des peuples à disposer d`eux-mêmes; (...) Ref. N° AL CAF 2/2021, 28 September 2021, (Jelena Aparac, UN independent expert on mercenaries) https://spcommreports.ohchr.org/TMResultsBase/DownLoadPublicCommunicationFile?gId=26626, accessed: 9 January 2023.

55 See also *Treasury Sanctions Russian Proxy Wagner Group as a Transnational Criminal Organization*, US Department of the Treasury, https://home.treasury.gov/news/press-releases/jy1220, accessed: 9 January 2023. 'Treasury is concurrently redesignating the Wagner Group pursuant to E.O. 13667 for being responsible for or complicit in, or having engaged in, the targeting of women, children, or any civilians through the commission of acts of violence, or abduction, forced displacement, or attacks on schools, hospitals, religious sites, or locations where civilians are seeking refuge, or through conduct that would constitute a serious abuse or violation of human rights or a violation of international humanitarian law in relation to the CAR.'

56 Picco, Enrica, 'Ten Years After the Coup, Is the Central African Republic Facing Another Major Crisis?', *ICG*, 22 March 2023. https://www.crisisgroup.org/africa/central-africa/central-african-republic/dix-ans-apres-le-coup-detat-la-republique, accessed: 20 March 2023.

57 Nzilo Alain, 'Les pratiques de torture des mercenaires de Wagner à Bangui', *Corbeau News*, 5 May 2023 https://corbeaunews-centrafrique.org/revelations-choquantes-sur-les-pratiques-de-torture-des-mercenaires-de-wagner-a-bangui-lune-des-victimes-temoigne/, accessed: 28 May 2023.

58 Olivier Mathieu, 'Centrafrique-Russie: qui est Vitali Perfilev, le patron de Wagner à Bangui?', 1 April 2022. https://www.jeuneafrique.com/1334939/politique/centrafrique-russie-qui-est-vitali-perfilev-le-patron-de-wagner-a-bangui/

59 Prigozhin accused French intelligence services of being behind the attack and declared France to be a 'state sponsor of terrorism.' Then a month later, on 8 April, Prigozhin spoke again about his right-hand man in a letter addressed to President Emmanuel Macron. Mathieu Olivier: 'Wagner's Dmitri Sytyi, Prigozhin's right-hand man, back in Bangui', *The Africa report*, 2 May 2023, https://www.theafricareport.com/304999/wagners-dmitri-sytyi-prigozhins-right-hand-man-back-in-bangui/, accessed: 28 May 2023.

60 Moïse Banafio, 'Entrée en action du mirage de Wagner', CNC *Corbeau News Centrafrique*, 31 January 2023, https://corbeaunews-centrafrique.org/centrafrique-entree-en-action-du-mirage-de-wagner-des-bombardements-effectues/, accessed: 20 March 2023.

61 *Wagner, les hommes de l`ombre de Poutine* (documentary).

62 Alexandre Ivanov <...> vient de publier une décalration sur l`explosion d`une mine vers Niem-Yéléwa qui a fait 3 morts et 5 blessés graves ', *Le Potentiel Centrafricaine.com*, 25 April 2023, https://lepotentielcentrafricain.com/alexandre-ivanov-chef-de-la-communaute-des-officiers-pour-la-securite-international-cosi-et-le-representant-des-instructeurs-russes-en-republique-centrafricaine-vient-de-publier-une-declaration-su/ (About the neutrality of *Le Potentiel* see Ancir Ilab : 'Central African Republic: Which news sources are pro-Russian and anti-Russian?', *Medium.com,* 13 January 2022, https://medium.com/african-c-i-r/friend-or-foe-how-the-central-african-republics-media-reports-on-russia-9c6496729de7, accessed: 20 March 2023.

63 Alexander Ivanov is a veteran who served in the Russian Armed Forces for 33 years, he not only has combat experience,

but is also an accomplished teacher, which is very important for a leader of an organisation specialising in training and educational support. As head of COSI, he acts as the official representative of Russian specialists working on the territory of the Central African Republic. 'A propos d`Alexandre Ivanov', *Officers Union*`s website, https://officersunion.org/a-propos-dalexandre-ivanov/, accessed: 20 March 2023.

64 'Centrafrique: arrivée de nouveaux mercenaires de Wagner en prévision du référendum constitutionnel', *Le Monde,* 17 July 2023. https://www.lemonde.fr/afrique/article/2023/07/17/centrafrique-arrivee-de-nouveaux-mercenaires-de-wagner-en-prevision-du-referendum-constitutionnel_6182298_3212.html, accessed: 17 July 2023.

65 Cyril Bensimon, 'How Wagner strengthened its control in the Central African Republic, despite the war in Ukraine', *LeMonde.fr*, 29 June 2023, https://www.lemonde.fr/en/le-monde-africa/article/2023/06/29/how-wagner-strengthened-its-control-in-the-central-african-republic-despite-the-war-in-ukraine_6039284_124.html, accessed: 17 July 2023.

66 Alain Nzilo, 'Début de l'entraînement de la milice AZANDE ANI KPI GBE par des mercenaires russes', *Corbeaunews*, 26 March 2024. https://corbeaunews-centrafrique.org/debut-de-lentrainement-de-la-milice-azande-ani-kpi-gbe-par-des-mercenaires-russes/

67 'Populist civil society, the Wagner Group, and post-coup politics in Mali', *West African Papers*, no. 36, July, 2022.

68 Ramani, *Russia in Africa*, pp. 281–285; Nedele, 'The Long Arm(s) of the State', pp. 27–28.

69 Between October 2020 – May 2021, Sadio attended military training in Russia and studied at the Moscow War School.

70 Of course, the presence of the Russians did not remain a secret. Hungarian and other soldiers serving in the EUTM Mali operation also met the members of the Wagner Group in several cases, of which they informed their superiors, but they did not want a clash with the Russians, so they tried to avoid them. Interview with Hungarian and French officers of EUTM MALI and another officer from MINUSMA, who requested anonymity.

71 Heinemann-Grüder, Aris, *Russian Analytical Digest*, 4.; Nedele, 'The Long Arm(s) of the State', p. 29.

72 Ramani, *Russia in Africa*, p. 286.

73 Wagner, les mercenaires de Poutine (documentary), Benoit Sarrade and Malick Konaté, BFMTV, 22 October 2022.

74 Ramani, *Russia in Africa*, pp. 311–313.

75 Jean-Michel Bos, 'Wagner coûte une fortune aux Etats africains', *Deutsche Welle*, 18 March 2023, https://www.dw.com/fr/wagner-co%C3%BBte-fortune-etats-africains/a-64987135, accessed: 20 March 2023.

76 Wagner, les mercenaires de Poutine.

77 It is interesting to note that having learned from the success of the Wagner propaganda, mainly in Africa, the French also started to build a similar IT propaganda network in Africa, partially using Prigozhin`s methods, but with some delay. Later in October 2021, the strategic document 'IT Wrestling for influence' (*Lutte Informatique d`Influence, L2l*) was developed.) The French also created fake Facebook profiles in order to spread information about Russian and Wagner activities in Africa, sometimes somewhat true, sometimes of dubious reliability, or using manipulative content and images. The results of Operation Barkhane were advertised. In any case, France lost the first part of the 'IT war' when in December 2020 Facebook deleted 84 fake Facebook accounts, six fake Facebook pages, and nine fake Facebook groups of the French 'secret operation' on the grounds that they had fake content and could be linked to the French Ministry of Defence. The French IT operation was characterised by amateurism and remained marginal, and it reached approximately only 6,000 people. They made such amateurish mistakes that they used a photo of Muhammad Ali for one of the main profiles (Martin Kossipé). Nataniel Gleicher, 'Removing Coordinated Inauthentic Behavior from France and Russia', *Meta/Facebook*, 15 December 2020. https://about.fb.com/news/2020/12/removing-coordinated-inauthentic-behavior-france-russia/, accessed: 20 March 2023; and Wagner, les mercenaires de Poutine.

78 A. I. Türke, 'Macron elnök Afrika-politikája a Száhel-szaharai övezetben' (French Military Operations in the Sahel, 2017–2022), *Honvédségi Szemle*, 1/2023, pp. 41–62.

79 Benjamin Roger, 'Au Mali, la ruée vers l'or des mercenaires de Wagner', *Jeuneafrique*, 20 June 2023. https://www.jeuneafrique.com/1451811/politique/au-mali-la-ruee-vers-lor-des-mercenaires-de-wagner/ accessed: 17 July 2023.

80 Benjamin Roger, 'Mali: comment Wagner compte faire main basse sur des mines d'or', *Missionnaires d`Afrique, Mafrwestafrica.net*, September 7, 2022. https://www.mafrwestafrica.net/vu-au-sud-vu-du-sud/6785-wagner-au-mali, accessed: 20 March 2023.

81 Mine. 'Le Mali pourrait devenir le premier producteur de lithium d'Afrique de l'Ouest, Le Mali pourrait devenir un géant de la production de lithium, ce métal indispensable aux économies modernes, friandes de batteries électriques. Un projet d'exploitation d'une mine par un consortium australo-chinois pourrait, à terme, hisser le pays parmi les principaux producteurs africains', *Courrier International*, 5 January 2022, https://www.courrierinternational.com/article/mine-le-mali-pourrait-devenir-le-premier-producteur-de-lithium-dafrique-de-louest, accessed: 23 July 2023.

82 Paul Melley, 'Was Ukraine's role in big Wagner defeat an own goal in Africa?', *BBC*, 12 August 2024, https://www.bbc.com/news/articles/c78ld18lgr9o

83 Ramani, *Russia in Africa*, p. 202.

84 Ramani, *Russia in Africa*, pp. 313–314.

85 'Propagande anti-française en Afrique: nouveau clip prorusse', *TV5MONDE Info*, Januar 22, 2023, https://www.youtube.com/watch?v=Cd0sAmVRQIs, accessed: 20 March 2023.

86 Matteo Maillard, 'Au Burkina Faso, «Libération» visé par une agence de propagande proche de Wagner', *Libération,* 12 April 2023, https://www.liberation.fr/international/afrique/au-burkina-faso-liberation-vise-par-une-agence-de-propagande-proche-de-wagner-20230412_JYPBVOFAXJGEBLQULBUU2NTV7Q/, accessed: 27 July 2023.

87 'US documents raise concerns over Russia's Wagner in Burkina Faso', (Youtube podcast), *Al Jazeera English,* April 15, 2023, https://www.youtube.com/watch?v=RK7GQTewBhw, accessed: 27 July 2023.

88 Scott N. Romaniuk and János Besenyő, 'Wagner Mercenaries: A Potential Lifeline for the Niger Junta', *Geopolitical Monitor*, 14 August 2023, https://www.geopoliticalmonitor.com/wagner-mercenaries-a-potential-lifeline-for-the-niger-junta/ accessed: 15 August 2023.

89 Damiba previously attended an American intelligence training course in Senegal. American policy has severed official relations with the political leadership based on Article 7008, but it is increasing its presence in the region due to Russian expansion. See Nicolas Beau, 'Les Etats Unis s'impliquent au Burkina Faso', *Mondafrique.com*, April 10, 2023, https://mondafrique.com/les-etats-unis-simpliquent-au-burkina-faso/, accessed: 27 July 2023.

90 'Dossier 17: Venezuela and hybrid wars in Latin America', *Journal of Global Faultlines* 6, no. 1 (August 2019), pp. 70–89, https://doi.org/10.13169/jglobfaul.6.1.0070, accessed: 9 January 2023.

91 John E. Herbst, Jason Marczak, 'Russia's Intervention in Venezuela: What's at Stake?', *Atlantic Council's Eurasia Center, Policy Brief*, September, 2019, https://www.atlanticcouncil.org/wp-content/uploads/2019/09/Russia-Venezuela-Policy-Brief.pdf; Carlos Malamud Rikles, Rogelio Núñez Castellano, 'Russia in Latin America: Variable Geometry of a Secondary Actor with Protagonist Aspirations', *Peruvian Army Center for Strategic Studies (CEEEP)*, 22 December 2022, https://ceeep.mil.pe/2022/12/22/russia-in-latin-america-variable-geometry-of-a-secondary-actor-with-protagonist-aspirations/?lang=en; Evan Ellis, Russia's Latest Return to Latin America, Global Americans, 19 January 2022, https://theglobalamericans.org/2022/01/russia-return-latin-america/, accessed: 9 January 2023.

92 'Sotrudniki rossiyskoy CHVK prileteli v Venesuelu okhranyat' Maduro', Dzen, 25 January 2019, https://dzen.ru/a/XEtvyKkejACsNEtN, accessed: 9 January 2023.

93 Maria Tsvetkova, Anton Zverev, 'Exclusive: Kremlin-linked contractors help guard Venezuela's Maduro – sources', *Reuters*, 25 January 2019, https://www.reuters.com/article/us-venezuela-politics-russia-exclusive-idUSKCN1PJ22M; Sergey Sukhankin, 'Russian mercenaries on the march: next stop Venezuela? The European Council on Foreign Relations', 1 February 2019, https://ecfr.eu/article/commentary_russian_mercenaries_on_the_march_next_stop_venezuela/, accessed: 9 January 2023.

94 Petersohn, pp. 106–128, Inigo Camilleri De Castanedo, 'Russian Paramilitary Presence in Venezuela?' *Grey Dynamics*, April 15, 2021, https://greydynamics.com/russian-paramilitary-presence-in-venezuela/, accessed: 9 January 2023.

95 'Russia's use of its private military companies', *Strategic Comments* 26, no. 10 (2020) vii-viii, DOI: 10.1080/13567888.2020.1868812; Jones et al., 'Russia's Corporate Soldiers', pp. 17, 20.

96 'Geopolitical debts. Why Russia is really sending military advisers and other specialists to Venezuela', *Medusa*, July 29, 2019, https://meduza.io/en/feature/2019/07/29/geopolitical-debts; Inigo Camilleri De Castanedo, 'Colectivos: Maduro's Venezuelan Militias', *Grey Dynamics*, 1 January 2022, https://greydynamics.com/colectivos-maduros-venezuelan-militias/, accessed: 9 January 2023.

97 'CHVK 'Vagnera' unichtozhila 93 amerikanskikh nayemnika v Venesuele', *Mirtesen*, 10 January 2020, https://armij.mirtesen.ru/blog/43164174444/CHVK-Vagnera-unichtozhila-93-amerikanskih-nayemnika-v-Venesuele; 'Venezuela: Former American soldiers jailed over failed coup', *BBC*, August 8, 2020, https://www.bbc.com/news/world-latin-america-53686509; Kevin T. Dugan, 'Inside Operation Gideon, a Coup Gone Very Wrong, Why did three American ex-Special Forces soldiers try to overthrow the Venezuelan government?', *Rolling Stone*, December 6, 2020, https://www.rollingstone.com/culture/culture-features/venezuela-operation-gideon-coup-jordan-goudreau-1098590/, accessed: 9 January 2023.

98 Steve Inskeep, 'Examining the Wagner Group, a private military company that Russia has relied on', *NPR*, 6 February 2023, https://www.npr.org/2023/02/06/1154739417/examining-the-wagner-group-a-private-military-company-that-russia-has-relied-on, accessed: 20 March 2023.

99 Inigo Camilleri De Castanedo, Russian Paramilitary Presence in Venezuela?

100 Akimenko Keir, 'Use and Utility of Russia's Private Military Companies'.

101 Sean Lyngaas, 'Leaked documents reveal heightened US anxiety over Russian and Chinese influence in Africa and Latin America', *CNN*, 13 April, 2023, https://edition.cnn.com/2023/04/13/politics/classified-leaks-pentagon-china-russia-africa/index.html, accessed: 20 March 2023.

102 Brian Katz, Seth G. Jones, Catria Doxsee and Nicholas Harrington, 'Moscow's Mercenary Wars: The Expansion of Russian Private Military Companies', *CSIS* (*Center for Strategic & International Studies*), September 2020, https://russianpmcs.csis.org/; David Lewis, John Heathershaw, Nick Megoran, 'Illiberal peace? Authoritarian modes of conflict management', *Cooperation and Conflict*, Vol.53(4), pp. 486–506.

103 'Army Relations between Russia - Sri Lanka Open up Training Slots for Armed Forces', *news.lk*, August 10, 2019, https://www.news.lk/news/political-current-affairs/item/26618-army-relations-between-russia-sri-lanka-open-up-training-slots-for-armed-forces; Russia offers training facilitates to Sri Lankan military, assistance to improve air operation capabilities, Feb 4, 2020, Colombo Page, http://www.colombopage.com/archive_20A/Feb04_1580756944CH.php; Rahul Kumar, 'Russia, Sri Lanka strengthen military relations with Sri Lankan general's Moscow visit', *India Narrative*, 28 October 2021, https://www.indianarrative.com/world-news/russia-sri-lanka-strengthen-military-relations-with-sri-lankan-generals-moscow-visit-27172.html, accessed: 9 January 2023.

104 Åse Gilje Østensen, Tor Bukkvoll, 'Russian Use of Private Military and Security Companies – the implications for European and Norwegian Security', *Norwegian Defence Research Establishment (FFI), FFI-RAPPORT* 18/01300, 11 September 2018, https://www.cmi.no/publications/6637-russian-use-of-private-military-and-security; Seth G. Jones, Catrina Doxsee, Brian Katz, Eric McQueen and Joe Moye, 'Russia's Corporate Soldiers, The Global Expansion of Russia's Private Military Companies', *Center for Strategic and International Studies* (*CSIS*), A Report of the CSIS Transnational Threats Project, July, 2021, 15.; Semen Kabakaev, Elena Aleksieieva, Fedor Morozov, Russian Private Military Companies: How Kremlin's Mercenaries Are Trained, '*Security and Cooperation in Ukraine*' - *Project "STOPTERROR"* https://s3images.coroflot.com/user_files/individual_files/695494_KwOPMh3oKQguM9bW4k0QoSST0.pdf

105 Candace Rondeaux, 'Decoding the Wagner Group: Analysing the Role of Private Military Security Contractors in Russian Proxy Warfare', *New America*, November,

2019, newamerica.org/international-security/reports/decoding-wagner-group-analyzing-role-private-military-securitycontractors-russian-proxy-warfare/, accessed: 9 January 2023.

106 Kanat Altynbayev, 'Russia's reliance on private military contractors raises alarm worldwide', *Caravanserai*, 11 December 2020, https://central.asia-news.com/en_GB/articles/cnmi_ca/features/2020/12/11/feature-01; 'Project VEGA: a new Russian PMC. The story of a hybrid PMC operating in the era of hybrid warfare', *Cyprus Daily News*, 20 December 2019, https://cyprus-daily.news/project-vega-a-new-russian-pmc-the-story-of-a-hybrid-pmc-operating-in-the-era-of-hybrid-warfare/, accessed: 9 January 2023.

107 'Catalog of Russian PMCs: 37 private military companies of the Russian Federation', *Molfar Global*, https://www.molfar.global/en-blog/catalog-of-russian-pmcs; 'Band of Brothers: The Wagner Group and the Russian State', *Center for Strategic and International Studies*, September 21, 2020, https://www.csis.org/blogs/post-soviet-post/band-brothers-wagner-group-and-russian-state; Anna Maria Dyner, 'The Role of Private Military Contractors in Russian Foreign Policy', Polish Institute of International Affairs, 4 May 2018, https://pism.pl/publications/The_Role_of_Private_Military_Contractors_in_Russian_Foreign_Policy

108 Candace Rondeaux, 'Decoding the Wagner Group: Analysing the Role of Private Military Security Contractors in Russian Proxy Warfare', *New America*, November, 2019, newamerica.org/international-security/reports/decoding-wagner-group-analyzing-role-private-military-securitycontractors-russian-proxy-warfare/, accessed: 9 January 2023.

109 Andrey Gubin, Russia-Sri Lanka Relations, The Eurasian Role of the 'Emerald Island', *Valdai Club*, 21 April 2022, https://valdaiclub.com/a/highlights/russia-sri-lanka-relations-the-eurasian-role/, accessed: 9 January 2023.

## Chapter 2

1 'To die for Bashar al-Assad', Fontanka.ru, 24 January 2014.

2 Jones et al., 'Russia's Corporate Soldiers', p. 34.; Sarah Fainberg, 'Russian Spetsnaz, Contractors and Volunteers in the Syrian Conflict', *Russie.Nei.Visions*, *Ifri*, no. 105, December, 2017, https://www.ifri.org/en/publications/notes-de-lifri/russieneivisions/russian-spetsnaz-contractors-and-volunteers-syrian; accessed: 9 January 2023.; James Kenneth Wither, 'Outsourcing warfare: Proxy forces in contemporary armed conflicts', *Security and Defence Quarterly* 31, no. 4 (2022), pp. 17–34.

3 McFate, *Mercenaries and War*, p. 3.; Keir and Akimenko, Guzansky, Marshall: 'Outsourcing warfare'; What losses PMC Wagner suffered in Syria, *Fontanka*, 22.08.2017, https://web.archive.org/web/20171008094928/http://rusletter.com/articles/what_losses_pmc_wagner_suffered_in_syria, accessed: 9 January 2023.

4 Candace Rondeaux, 'Decoding the Wagner Group: Analyzing the Role of Private Military Security Contractors in Russian Proxy Warfare', *New America*, November, 2019, newamerica.org/international-security/reports/decoding-wagner-group-analyzing-role-private-military-securitycontractors-russian-proxy-warfare/, accessed: 9 January 2023.

5 Ruslan Leviev, 'Shestoy pogibshiy v Sirii rossiyskiy voyennosluzhashchiy', Conflict Intelligence Team, 22.03.2016, https://citeam.org/sixth-ru-serviceman-killed-in-syria/; Ruslan Leviev, 'IGIL zayavilo ob ubiystve trokh rossiyskikh soldat', Conflict Intelligence Team, 23.06.2016, https://citeam.org/isis-claimed-they-killed-three-russian-soldiers/; Ruslan Leviev, 'V khode boya pod Pal'miroy pogib rossiyskiy morpekh', Conflict Intelligence Team, 19.06.2016, https://citeam.org/russian-marine-died/; Ruslan Leviev, 'Sekretnyye poteri Sil spetsial'nykh operatsiy', Conflict Intelligence Team, 18.08.2016, https://citeam.org/russian-sof-soldiers/; Ruslan Leviev, 'Na siriyskom fronte bez peremen: rossiyskiye SSO poteryali yeshcho odnogo boytsa', Conflict Intelligence Team, 07.02.2019, https://citeam.org/ru-sof-in-syria-2019/, accessed: 9 January 2023.

6 Ruslan Pukhov, 'Moscow-based think tank director: Russia's unexpected military victory in Syria', *Defence News,* 11 December 2017, https://www.defensenews.com/outlook/2017/12/11/moscow-based-think-tank-director-russias-unexpected-military-victory-in-syria/, accessed: 9 January 2023.

7 'What losses PMC Wagner suffered in Syria', *Fontanka*, 22.08.2017, https://web.archive.org/web/20171008094928/http://rusletter.com/articles/what_losses_pmc_wagner_suffered_in_syria, accessed: 9 January 2023.

8 John W. Parker, 'Putin's Syrian Gambit: Sharper Elbows, Bigger Footprint, Stickier Wicket', Institute for National Strategic Studies Strategic Perspectives, No. 25. Washington, D.C.: National Defense University Press, https://ndupress.ndu.edu/Media/News/Article/1239376/putins-syrian-gambit-sharper-elbows-bigger-footprint-stickier-wicket/, accessed: 9 January 2023.

9 Thomas Grove, 'Up to Nine Russian Contractors Die in Syria, Experts Say', *The Wall Street Journal*, Dec. 18, 2015, https://www.wsj.com/articles/up-to-nine-russian-contractors-die-in-syria-experts-say-1450467757, accessed: 9 January 2023.

10 Catherine A. Fitzpatrick, 'How Many Russian Soldiers Have Died in Syria?' *Daily Beast*, Jun. 21, 2016, https://www.thedailybeast.com/how-many-russian-soldiers-have-died-in-syria; Pierre Vaux, 'Fontanka Investigates Russian Mercenaries Dying For Putin In Syria And Ukraine', *The Interpreter*, March 29, 2016, https://www.interpretermag.com/fontanka-investigates-russian-mercenaries-dying-for-putin-in-syria-and-ukraine/; 'Oni srazhalis' za Pal'miru', *Fontanka,* 29 марта 2016, https://www.fontanka.ru/2016/03/28/171/, accessed: 9 January 2023.

11 Ruslan Leviev, 'Oni opyat' srazhalis' za Pal'miru: boytsy 'CHVK Vagnera', pogibshiye v boyakh s IG', Conflict Intelligence Team, 10.03.2017, https://citeam.org/pmc-wagner-palmyra-2/; Ruslan Leviev, 'Spisok poter' CHVK Vagnera v Sirii rastot', Conflict Intelligence Team, 16.10.2017, https://citeam.org/wagner-kia-list/; 'What losses PMC Wagner suffered in Syria', *Fontanka*, 22.08.2017, https://web.archive.org/web/20171008094928/http://rusletter.com/articles/what_losses_pmc_wagner_suffered_in_syria, accessed: 9 January 2023.

12 Ruslan Leviev, 'Rodstvennikam nayemnikov 'CHVK Vagnera' mesyatsami ne soobshchayut ob ikh gibeli', 18.12.2017. https://citeam.org/ru-mercenaries-killed-in-syria/, accessed: 9 January 2023.

13 Heinemann-Grüder, Aris, *Russian Analytical Digest*, 3.; Sergey Sukhankin, 'Russian PMCs in the Syrian Civil War: From Slavonic Corps to Wagner Group and Beyond', December 18, 2019, https://jamestown.org/program/russian-pmcs-in-the-syrian-civil-war-from-slavonic-corps-to-wagner-group-and-beyond/; 'Pogibshiy v Sirii rossiyanin Slyshkin sluzhil v gruppe Vagnera', *RBC,* 6 March 2017, https://www.rbc.ru/politics/06/03/2017/58bd3bc49a7947df4da2e17a; 'Nayemnik CHVK Vagnera: Polovinu lyudey 'nakrylo' pryamo v mashinakh', Charter97.org, 7 June 2023, https://charter97.org/ru/news/1970/1/1/315888/, accessed: 9 January 2023. The 'Syrian Democratic Forces' was a front of the Kurdish Workers Party's (PKK) Syrian branch, the 'People's Defence Units' (abbreviated as YPG): it was designated the 'Syrian Democratic Forces' on advice from the CENTOM and the United States Special Operations Command (SOCOM) in order to circumnavigate US laws which designated the PKK (and all the affiliated organisations) a 'terrorist organisation', and thus strictly prohibited any kind of cooperation or provision of support. For details about this process, see the interview with General Raymond Thomas (contemporary commander of the SOCOM) to the Aspen Institute Security Forum, on 21 July 2017, available on https://www.youtube.com/watch?v=kVZCIel_2Xw & Shawn Snow, 'SOCOM Commander: US asked YPG to re-brand because of alleged Terrorist Link', *MilitaryTimes.com*, 22 July 2017.

14 'Spisok Vagnera', *Fontanka*, August 21, 2017, https://www.fontanka.ru/2017/08/18/075/, accessed: 9 January 2023.

15 Michael Weiss, Mattias Carlsson, Alnahhal Saeed, 'A Syrian Army Deserter Was Savagely Killed by Putin's Wagner. Now His Family Seek Justice in Russia', *News Lines Magazine*, December 22, 2021. https://newlinesmag.com/reportage/family-seek-justice-in-russia-fo-syrian-army-deserter-was-savagely-killed-by-putins-wagner/, accessed: 9 January 2023.

16 Wagner, les mercenaires de la Russie (1/2).

17 *Regulation (EU) No 2021/2195 of 13 December 2021 implementing Regulation (EU) 2020/1998 concerning restrictive measures against serious human rights violations and abuses*, https://eur-lex.europa.eu/legal-content/EN/TXT/?uri=CELEX:32021R2195.

18 Niko Vorobyov, 'Shrouded in secrecy for years, Russia's Wagner Group opens up, The mysterious network of mercenaries is embracing an ever-public image as the war on Ukraine drags on', Aljazeera, 10 August 2022, https://www.aljazeera.com/news/2022/8/10/wagner-private-group-now-an-extension-of-russias-military, accessed: 23 July 2023.

19 Wagner, 'les mercenaires de la Russie' (1/2), (documentary), Benoit Bringer, ARTE, 2023.

20 Andrew Osborn, 'Putin, in Syria, says mission accomplished, orders partial Russian pull-out', *Reuters*, December 11, 2017, https://www.reuters.com/article/us-mideast-crisis-syria-russia-putin-idUSKBN1E50X1, accessed: 9 January 2023.

21 Leonid M. Issaev, 'What is After Russia's Military Withdrawal From Syria?', Al Jazeera Centre for Studies, February 2018, https://studies.aljazeera.net/en/reports/2018/02/russia-military-withdrawal-syria-180205061719003.html; Moritz Pieper, 'Russia's decision to withdraw from Syria isn't about how to leave, but how to stay', *The Conversation*, December 15, 2017, https://theconversation.com/russias-decision-to-withdraw-from-syria-isnt-about-how-to-leave-but-how-to-stay-89095, accessed: 9 January 2023.

22 News Transcript: Department of Defense Press Briefing by Lieutenant-General Harrigian, via teleconference from Al Udeid Airbase, Qatar, 15 February 2018; 'Russian Mercenary Boss spoke with Kremlin before attacking US Forces in Syria, Intel claims', *The Telegraph*, 23 February 2018; 'Putin Ally said to be in touch with Kremlin, Assad before his mercenaries attacked US Troops', *The Washington Post*, 22 February 2018.

23 Kevin Maurer, 'Special Forces Soldiers Reveal First Details of Battle With Russian Mercenaries in Syria', *The Warhorse*, 11 May 2023, https://thewarhorse.org/special-forces-soldiers-reveal-first-details-of-battle-with-russian-mercenaries-in-syria/, accessed: 11 May 2023.

24 SDF release, 8 February 2018; Syrian Reporters, Twitter post, 8 February 2018; Gabidullin, *Moi, Marat*, pp. 24–25.; Dyner, 'The Role of Private Military',; Wither, 'Outsourcing warfare', p. 22.; Galeotti, *The Weaponisation of Everything*, p. 41; Christoph Reuter, 'The Truth About the Russian Deaths in Syria', *Spiegel International*, 02.03.2018, https://www.spiegel.de/international/world/american-fury-the-truth-about-the-russian-deaths-in-syria-a-1196074.html; Anna Varfolomeeva, 'More than 200 Russians may have been killed in Coalition strikes against 'pro-regime' forces in Syria', The Defence Post, February 10, 2018, https://www.thedefensepost.com/2018/02/10/russians-killed-coalition-strikes-deir-ezzor-syria/; Mac Caltrider, 'That Time US Forces Tore Hundreds of Russian Wagner Group Mercenaries to Pieces in Syria', *Coffee or Die Magazine,* March 25, 2022, https://coffeeordie.com/wagner-group-syria-khasham, accessed: 9 January 2023.

25 'PMC Wagner Chief: 14 were killed in Syria', *PravdaReport*, 19 February 2018.

26 Kevin Maurer, Special Forces Soldiers Reveal First Details of Battle With Russian Mercenaries in Syria, *The Warhorse*, 11 May 2023, https://thewarhorse.org/special-forces-soldiers-reveal-first-details-of-battle-with-russian-mercenaries-in-syria/, accessed: 9 January 2023.

27 Fainberg, 'Russian Spetsnaz', Anna Nemtsova, 'A Russian Blackwater? Putin's Secret Soldiers in Ukraine and Syria', *The Daily Beast.* Jan. 02, 2018, https://www.thedailybeast.com/a-russian-blackwater-putins-secret-soldiers-in-ukraine-and-syria, accessed: 9 January 2023.

28 Anna Maria Dyner, 'The Role of Private Military Contractors in Russian Foreign Policy', *PISM Bulletin*, no. 64 (1135), May 4, 2018, https://www.ceeol.com/search/gray-literature-detail?id=852774., accessed: 9 January 2023, McFate, *Mercenaries*, p. 31, Jones et al., 'Russia's Corporate Soldiers', pp. 37–38.

29 'What losses PMC Wagner suffered in Syria', *Fontanka*, 22.08.2017, https://web.archive.org/web/20171008094928/http://rusletter.com/articles/what_losses_pmc_wagner_suffered_in_syria accessed: 9 January 2023.

30 Sergey Sukhankin, 'Russian Mercenaries Pour Into Africa and Suffer More Losses (Part One)', *Eurasia Daily Monitor* 17, no. 6, January 21, 2020, https://jamestown.org/program/russian-mercenaries-pour-into-africa-and-suffer-more-losses-part-one/.; Galeotti, *The Weaponisation of Everything*, p. 55.

31 Ruslan Pukhov, 'Moscow-based think tank director: Russia's unexpected military victory in Syria', *Defence News,* Dec 11, 2017, https://www.defensenews.com/outlook/2017/12/11/moscow-based-think-tank-director-russias-unexpected-military-victory-in-syria/, accessed: 9 January 2023.

32 Sergey Khazov-Kassia, Proyekt 'Myasorubka'. Rasskazyvayut tri komandira 'CHVK Vagnera', Radio Free Europe, Radio Liberty, 7 March 2018, https://www.svoboda.org/a/29084090.html, accessed: 9 January 2023.

33 U. Petersohn, 'The anti-mercenary norm and the market for combat force', *International Journal,* 76(1), pp. 106–128, https://doi.org/10.1177/0020702021994519, accessed: 9 January 2023.

34 Bill Bostock, 'Video shows the inside of an abandoned US camp in Syria taken over by Russian mercenaries', *Business Insider,* Oct 15, 2019, https://www.businessinsider.com/russia-mercenaries-seize-abandoned-us-base-syria-video-2019-10, accessed: 9 January 2023.

35 Shawn Snow, 'US troops have been squaring off with Russian contractors in Syria raising worries of wider conflict', *ArmyTimes,* Feb 6, 2020, https://www.armytimes.com/flashpoints/2020/02/06/us-troops-have-been-squaring-off-with-russian-contractors-in-syria-raising-worries-of-wider-conflict/, accessed: 9 January 2023.

36 Zana Omar, Rikar Hussein, 'US Forces Block Another Russian Convoy as Tensions Rise in Northeast Syria', *VoaNews,* 31 January 2020, https://www.voanews.com/a/extremism-watch_us-forces-block-another-russian-convoy-tensions-rise-northeast-syria/6183533.html; 'Russian Troops Block U.S. Military Convoy in Syria', *The Moscow Times,* May 14, 2021, https://www.themoscowtimes.com/2021/05/14/russian-troops-block-us-military-convoy-in-syria-a73890, accessed: 9 January 2023.

37 Ryan Browne, Barbara Starr, 'Pentagon slams Russia for 'provocative and aggressive behaviour' that injured US troops in Syria', *CNN Politics*, August 27, 2020, https://edition.cnn.com/2020/08/27/politics/pentagon-russia-syria/index.html, accessed: 9 January 2023.

38 Dar'ya Ryabova, 'Politolog: v Sirii uzhestochilis' boi posle vyvoda CHVK 'Vagnera', *URA,* 11 January 2021, https://ura.news/news/1052466533, accessed: 9 January 2023.

39 'Supported by Regime forces. Wagner and Fatemiyoun launch military campaign against ISIS in Syrian desert', *The Syrian Observatory for Human Rights*, Dec 22, 2021, https://www.syriahr.com/en/231799/, accessed: 9 January 2023.

40 Gregory Waters: 'ISIS beats back Wagner offensive in central Syria', *Middle East Institute*, April 21, 2023, https://www.mei.edu/publications/isis-beats-back-wagner-offensive-central-syria, accessed: 21 April 2023.

41 Jason Blazakis, Colin P. Clarke, Naureen Chowdhury Fink, Sean Steinberg, 'WAGNER GROUP: The Evolution of a Private Army', *The Soufan Center*, June 2023, https://thesoufancenter.org/wp-content/uploads/2023/06/TSC-Special-Report-The-Wagner-Group-The-Evolution-Of-Putins-Private-Army.pdf; 'New Testimonies: Russia Continues to Deploy Syrian Mercenaries to Ukraine, Syrians for Truth and Justice', December 20, 2022, https://stj-sy.org/en/new-testimonies-russia-continues-to-deploy-syrian-mercenaries-to-ukraine/, accessed: 9 January 2023.

42 'Ukraine's consequences are finally spreading to Syria', *War on the Rocks*, January 10, 2023, https://warontherocks.com/2023/01/ukraines-consequences-are-finally-spreading-to-syria/, accessed: 20 March 2023.

## Chapter 3

1 Alessandro Sereni, 'A Game of Shadows: Russian, American, and Chinese Private Military and Security Companies', *SAGE International, Australia*, 22 May 2021, p. 2.

2 Kaunert Foley, 'Russian Private Military and Ukraine', pp. 172–192.; Mark Galeotti, *The Weaponisation of Everything: A Field Guide to the New Way of War* (New Haven: Yale University Press, 2022), p. 55.

3 'Teper' u 'Vagnera' tri znakovykh pobedy — Popasnaya, Soledar i Artomovsk', *Rusvesna*, May 21, 2023, https://rusvesna.su/news/1684593557, accessed: 20 March 2023.

4 'Shoygu: v ramkakh mobilizatsii budet zadeystvovano okolo 1% mobilizatsionnogo resursa, Ministr oborony podcherknul, chto u Rossii ogromnyy mobilizatsionnyy resurs tekh, kto imeyet boyevoy opyt, voyennuyu spetsial'nost'', *TASS*, September 21, 2022, https://tass.ru/armiya-i-opk/15817251, accessed: 20 March 2023.

5 'As second mobilization looms, Russian men are staying put (for now), Russians have various views on an impending new draft — along with strategies to evade it', *Politico,* 4 February 2023, https://www.politico.eu/article/second-mobilization-russia-men-vladimir-putin-ukraine-war/, accessed: 20 July 2023; Jonathan Landay, 'Russia declares end of Ukraine mobilisation campaign, U.S. sending more arms', *Reuters*, 29 October 2022, https://www.reuters.com/world/europe/russia-hits-ukraine-homes-evacuates-kherson-warns-escalation-2022-10-24/, accessed: 20 July 2023; Mariya Panina: 'Mobilizatsiya: V Rossii sdelali zayavleniye v maye 2023', *Berdsk Online*, 24 May 2023, https://berdsk-online.ru/news/v-strane/mobilizacziya-v-rossii-sdelali-zayavlenie-v-mae-2023/, accessed: 20 July 2023.

6 'Ukraine finds stepping up mobilisation is not so easy, Military recruiters are accused of rough tactics as they try to boost the head count', *The Economist*, 26 February 2023, https://www.economist.com/europe/2023/02/26/ukraine-finds-stepping-up-mobilisation-is-not-so-easy, accessed: 20 July 2023; Matthew Luxmoore, 'A Year Into War, Ukraine Faces Challenges Mobilizing Troops, So far, Ukraine has managed to replenish its ranks. But some draft-age men are dodging mobilization. While polls show that support for Ukraine's defense effort remains high, the stock of willing volunteers now appears to be dwindling', *The Wall Street Journal*, 23 March 2023, https://www.wsj.com/articles/a-year-into-war-ukraine-faces-challenges-mobilizing-troops-64dcdc49, accessed: 20 July 2023; Aleksandr Kryzhanovskiy, 'Vseobshchaya mogilizatsiya: ukraintsam ne udastsya uklonit'sya ot prizyva', *Antifashist*, May 23, 2022, https://antifashist.com/item/vseobshhaya-mogilizaciya-ukraincam-ne-udastsya-uklonitsya-ot-prizyva.html, accessed: 20 March 2023.

7 'Peskov oproverg informatsiyu o planakh mobilizovat' million chelovek, Peskov nazval lozh'yu informatsiyu o planakh mobilizovat' million chelovek', *RIA*, 22 September 2022, https://ria.ru/20220922/mobilizatsiya-1818694689.html, accessed: 20 March 2023.

8 'Chernyshenko: boleye 70 tys. rossiyan zakhoteli zapisat'sya v dobrovol'tsy v ramkakh SVO, Pri etom na portale Gosuslug zapushchen servis dlya obzhalovaniya resheniya ob oshibochnoy chastichnoy mobilizatsii, otmetil zamestitel' predsedatelya pravitel'stva', *TASS*, October 4,

2022, https://tass.ru/armiya-i-opk/15946629, accessed: 20 March 2023.

9 'S yanvarya 2023 goda na kontraktnuyu sluzhbu v VS RF postupilo boleye 117 tysyach chelovek', *Antifashist*, May 19, 2023, https://antifashist.com/item/s-yanvarya-2023-goda-na-kontraktnuyu-sluzhbu-v-vs-rf-postupilo-bolee-117-tysyach-chelovek.html, accessed: 19 May 2023.

10 David Ehl, 'More than mercenaries: Russia's Wagner Group in Africa', *Deutsche Welle*, February 28, 2023, https://www.dw.com/en/more-than-mercenaries-russias-wagner-group-in-africa/a-64822234, accessed: 20 March 2023.

11 'Surovikin: poyezd tronulsya', *Antifashist*, 8 May 2023, https://antifashist.com/item/surovikin-poezd-tronulsya.html, accessed: 8 May 2023.

12 'Shoygu poruchil derzhat' na osobom kontrole snabzheniye sil v zone SVO', *Antifashist*, May 5, 2023, https://antifashist.com/item/shojgu-poruchil-derzhat-na-osobom-kontrole-snabzhenie-sil-v-zone-svo.html, accessed: 8 May 2023.

## Chapter 4

1 Gabidullin, pp. 298–316, 404–434.

2 Kaunert Foley, 'Russian Private Military and Ukraine', pp. 172–192.; 'Putin's Mercenaries on Tour: Mapping the Wagner Group's Global Activities', *T-Intelligence*, 2021, https://t-intell.com/2021/09/28/putins-mercenaries-on-tour-mapping-the-wagner-groups-global-activities/, accessed: 20 March 2023.

3 André Ballin, 'Vom Chefkiller zum Chefkoch, Dmitri Utkin war Berufssoldat, Söldnerkommandant – und ist nun General Manager der 'Concord Management & Consulting', die eine Reihe von Restaurants betreibt. Doch harmlos sind die Geschäfte der Firma nur auf den ersten Blick', *Handelsblatt*, 15 November 2017, https://www.handelsblatt.com/arts_und_style/aus-aller-welt/dmitri-utkin-vom-chefkiller-zum-chefkoch/20590186.html, accessed: 20 March 2023.

4 'Putin Chef's Kisses of Death: Russia's Shadow Army's State-Run Structure Exposed', *Bellingcat*, 14 August 2020, https://www.bellingcat.com/news/uk-and-europe/2020/08/14/pmc-structure-exposed/, accessed: 21 July 2023.

5 Alexandra Jousset, 'Les mercenaires de Wagner ont 'toujours été présents en Ukraine', selon l'autrice du documentaire 'Wagner, l'armée secrète de Poutine', Alexandra Jousset, autrice-réalisatrice du documentaire 'Wagner, l'armée secrète de Poutine', explique sur franceinfo que si la base centrale de Wagner est en Afrique, l'organisation, qui n'a pas d'existence juridique, a pour berceau l'Ukraine', *Radio France*, March 1, 2022, https://www.francetvinfo.fr/monde/europe/manifestations-en-ukraine/les-mercenaires-de-wagner-ont-toujours-ete-presents-en-ukraine-selon-l-autrice-du-documentaire-wagner-l-armee-secrete-de-poutine_4987635.html, accessed: 20 March 2023; Gabidullin, pp. 34–35, 41, 229.

6 Schemes & Systema, 'How Russia's GRU set up a Fake Private Military Company for its War in Ukraine', *rferl.org.*, 10 October 2023.

7 'Wagner Mercenaries with GRU-issued Passports: Validating SBU's Allegation', bellingcat.com, 30 January 2019.

8 Schemes & Systema, 'How Russia's GRU set up a Fake Private Military Company for its War in Ukraine', *rferl.org.*, 10 October 2023.

## Chapter 5

1 Maria Katamadze, 'Russia: Can Wagner head Yevgeny Prigozhin challenge Putin?', *Deutsche Welle*, February 22, 2023, https://www.dw.com/en/russia-can-wagner-head-yevgeny-prigozhin-challenge-putin/a-64744266.; 'Russian Proxy or Rogue Mercenary Army?, Situating the Wagner Group', *International Master Security, Intelligence and Strategic Studies (IMSISS)*, July, 2022.

2 Kimberly Marten, 'Russia's use of semi-state security forces: the case of the Wagner Group', *Post-Soviet Affairs* 35, no. 3 (2019), 4., DOI: 10.1080/1060586X.2019.1591142.

3 Preston Feinberg, *The fluctuating relationship between Russia and the Wagner Group* (Baltimore, Maryland: Johns Hopkins University, December 2020), and Grigoriy Petrovich, 'CHVK Vagnera – taynyye geroi nashego vremeni', *Moscow Forum*, 26 September 2022, https://forum-msk.info/threads/chvk-vagnera-tajnye-geroi-nashego-vremeni.5269/, accessed: 20 March 2023.

4 Luc Mathieu, Veronika Dorman, 'Mercenaires russes : du Donbass à Damas, des 'héros' pas assez discrets', *Liberation*, March 12, 2018, https://www.liberation.fr/planete/2018/03/12/mercenaires-russes-du-donbass-a-damas-des-heros-pas-assez-discrets_1635677/, accessed: 24 March 2023; Sergey Sukhankin, 'Russian PMCs in the Syrian Civil War: From Slavonic Corps to Wagner Group and Beyond', December 18, 2019, https://jamestown.org/program/russian-pmcs-in-the-syrian-civil-war-from-slavonic-corps-to-wagner-group-and-beyond/, accessed: 20 March 2023.

5 Marten.

6 Candace Rondeaux, 'Decoding the Wagner Group: Analyzing the Role of Private Military Security Contractors in Russian Proxy Warfare', *New America*, November 2019, newamerica.org/international-security/reports/decoding-wagner-group-analyzing-role-private-military-securitycontractors-russian-proxy-warfare/, accessed: 9 January 2023.

7 The Constitution of the Russian Federation, Constitution, 20 July 2023, http://www.constitution.ru/en/10003000-01.htm, accessed: 20 July 2023; 'Konstitutsiya Rossiyskoy Federatsii' (prinyata vsenarodnym golosovaniyem 12.12.1993 s izmeneniyami, odobrennymi v khode obshcherossiyskogo golosovaniya 01.07.2020), Stat'ya 13, *Consultant Plus*, 2023, https://www.consultant.ru/document/cons_doc LAW_28399/5b9338a7944b7701f-be63f48c943e8175be16462/, accessed: 20 March 2023; 'Ugolovnyy kodeks Rossiyskoy Federatsii' ot 13.06.1996 N 63-FZ (red. ot 14.04.2023), UK RF Stat'ya 208. Organizatsiya nezakonnogo vooruzhennogo formirovaniya ili uchastiye v nem, a ravno uchastiye v vooruzhennom konflikte ili voy-ennykh deystviyakh v tselyakh', *Consultant Plus*, 2023, https://www.consultant.ru/document/cons_doc_LAW_10699/ef3f3b-e211c40981d10e672287aa8c4b7c98987a/, accessed: 20 April 2023; Ugolovnyy kodeks Rossiyskoy Federatsii (s izmeneni-yami na 14 aprelya 2023 goda), Elektronnyy fond pravovy-kh i normativno-tekhnicheskikh dokumentov, April 2023, https://docs.cntd.ru/document/9017477, accessed: 20 April 2023.

8 Voyennyye kontrakty smogut zaklyuchat' s sudimymi i ogranichenno godnymi, Takzhe dokumentom predlozheno prodlit' predel'nyy vozrast prebyvaniya na voyennoy

sluzhbe v period mobilizatsii, voyennogo polozheniya ili v voyennoye vremya, Duma, 20 June 2023, http://duma.gov.ru/news/57342/, accessed: 20 June 2023; Gosduma prinyala zakon o prizyve osuzhdennykh na voyennuyu sluzhbu po kontraktu, Gosduma vo vtornik prinyala zakon o prizyve osuzhdennykh na voyennuyu sluzhbu po kontraktu, RIA, 20 June 2023, https://ria.ru/20230620/sluzhba-1879353424.html, accessed: 20 June 2023.

9 Russian State Duma official homepage: sozd.duma.gov.ru

10 Nathan Hodge, 'Wagner 'does not exist': Why Putin claims a rift in the mercenary group', *CNN*, 14 July 2023, https://edition.cnn.com/2023/07/14/europe/russia-putin-wagner-prigozhin-tensions-intl/index.html, accessed: 20 July 2023; 'Wagner PMC formally non-existent, Putin says — media, The president explained that Russia has no law on private military companies and, therefore, 'there is no such legal entity', *TASS*, 14 July 2023, https://tass.com/politics/1646675, accessed: 14 July 2023; 'Putin: CHVK 'Vagner' ne sushchestvuyet', *Antifashist*, 14 July 2023, https://antifashist.com/item/putin-chvk-vagner-ne-sushhestvuet.html, accessed: 14 July 2023.

11 OMON is the Special Purpose Mobile Unit (formerly the Ministry of Internal Affairs (MVD) troops), SOBR is the Special Rapid Response Unit of the National Guard of Russia, while the VDV are Russia's independent Airborne Forces branch.

12 'Wagner's Gold: How much do they pay for living and dead Mercenaries, how Russian Military Companies divide Africa, and who is behind the new PMC 'Patriot' (in Russian), tvrain.tv (https://tvrain.tv/teleshow/reportazh/chvk-467150/), 25 September 2013 and 'Industry Talk: The Slavonic Corps – a Russian PMC in Syria', FeralJundi.com, 14 January 2014.

13 Marten, pp. 12–16; Kiana Nedele, 'The Long Arm(s) of the State: The Role of the Wagner Group in Russia's Pivot to Africa, 2017–2022', *World Peace Foundation*, February, 2023, p. 12; '08.03.2023 CHVK Vagner', *Emigrating*, March 8, 2023, https://emigrating.ru/08-03-2023-chvk-vagner/, accessed: 20 March 2023. Notably, some French sources mention Utkin as also being the founder of the Slavonic Corps. However, this is rather questionable: Utkin did serve with that PMC in Syria, but by the time he did so, he would have already left the GRU. Alternatively, he might have been one of nine officers known to have been assigned to the Slavonic Corps at the time.

14 Nathaniel Reynolds, *Putin's Not-So-Secret Mercenaries: Patronage, Geopolitics, and the Wagner Group* (Washington D. C.: Carnegie Endowment for International Peace, 2019), p. 2.; Seth G. Jones, Catrina Doxsee, Brian Katz, Eric McQueen and Joe Moye, 'Russia's Corporate Soldiers, The Global Expansion of Russia's Private Military Companies', *Center for Strategic and International Studies (CSIS), A Report of the CSIS Transnational Threats Project*, July, 2021, pp. 15–16.

15 'Slavonic Corps returns to Syria' (in Russian), *Fontanka, ru*, 16 October 2015; Vladimir Dergachev & Ekaterina Zgirovskaya, 'Russian Mercenaries in the Battle for Palmyra' (in Russian), *Gazeta.ru.*, 24 March 2016.

16 'What Losses PMC Wagner suffered in Syria', *Fontanka.ru*, 22 August 2017.

17 'Putin's Chef's Kisses of Death', Bellingcat.com, 14 August 2020.

18 'Wagner, Russian Blackwater in Syria', *Yeni Safak*, 6 August 2017; Schemes & Systema, 'How Russia's GRU set up a Fake Private Military Company for its War in Ukraine', *rferl.org.*, 10 October 2023;

19 'Wagner PMC Commander Dmitry Utkin (a.k.a. 'Wagner') buried at Memorial Cemetery in Mytgishchi, *Meduza.io*, 31 August 2023.

## Chapter 6

1 Pertti Joenniemi, 'Two Models of Mercenarism; Historical and Contemporary', *Instant Research on Peace and Violence* 7, no. 3/4 (1977): pp. 184–196, https://www.jstor.org/stable/40724838.

2 Xenophon, *Anabasis*, https://www.fulltextarchive.com/book/Anabasis/

3 Matthew Trundle, *Greek Mercenaries: From the Late Archaic Period to Alexander* (London: Routledge, 2004), pp. 4, 16, 23, 36, 44–46.

4 Melanie Jonasch, *The Fight for Greek Sicily: Society, Politics, and Landscape* (Oxford: Oxbow Books, 2020), p. 160.

5 Trundle, pp. 6, 7–8, 43, 45.

6 Dexter Hoyos, *Carthage's Other Wars: Carthaginian Warfare Outside the 'Punic Wars' Against Rome* (Barnsley, Pen and Sword Books Limited, 2019), pp. 20–21, 25–31.

7 Jeremy Armstrong, *Early Roman Warfare: From the Regal Period to the First Punic War* (Barnsley, Pen and Sword, 2016), pp. 161–162; John Lazenby, *The First Punic War* (London: Routledge, 2016), pp. 102–106.

8 Hoyos, p. 5.

9 Peter Macdonald, *Soldiers of Fortune, The Twentieth Century Mercenary* (New York: Gallery Books, 1986), p. 8.

10 Sigfús Blöndal, *The Varangians of Byzantium* (Cambridge University Press, 2007), p. 20.

11 Blöndal, pp. 20–31, 54–102; Csete Katona, *Vikings of the Steppe: Scandinavians, Rus', and the Turkic World (c. 750–1050)* (London: Routledge, 2022), pp. 101–103.

12 Katona, pp. 104–107.

13 Adinel C. Dincă, 'Hungarian Mercenaries Serving the Pontifical State, A Vatican Source from 1362 and the Beginning of a Discussion', in: Andrea Fara (a cura di), *Italia ed Europa centroorientale tra Medioevo ed Età moderna. Economia, Società, Cultura* (Heidelberg: Heidelberg University Publishing 2022), (OnlineSchriften des DHI Rom. Neue Reihe | Pubblicazioni online del DHI Roma. Nuova serie, vol. 7), pp. 43–54. https://doi.org/10.17885/heiup.832.c13879; Giulia Morosini, 'The Body of the Condottiero A Link Between Physical Pain and Military Virtue as it was Interpreted in Renaissance Italy' in Jörg Rogge (ed.) *Killing and Being Killed: Bodies in Battle: Perspectives on Fighters in the Middle Ages*, (Bielefeld: transcript Verlag, 2017), pp. 165–198. https://doi.org/10.1515/9783839437834-010; Michael Mallett, 'Condottieri and Captains in Renaissance Italy' in: David J. B. Trim (ed), *The Chivalric Ethos and the Development of Military Professionalism* (BRILL, 2003), pp. 67–88, https://doi.org/10.1163/9789047400882_008; Michael Mallett, 'Condottieri' in: Eugenio Garin (ed), *Renaissance Characters* (Chicago: University of Chicago Press, 1997) pp. 22–45; David Murphy, *Condottiere 1300–1500: Infamous medieval mercenaries* (London: Bloomsbury Publishing, 2021); Attila Bárány, 'The Communion of English and Hungarian Mercenaries in Italy.' In Barta János (ed), *The First Millennium of Hungary in Europe* (Debrecen: Multiplex Media-Debrecen University Press, 2002), pp. 126–141.

14 Florio Banfi, *Hunyadi János itáliai tartózkodása* (Erdélyi Múzeum 5 (1934), pp. 262–272, http://epa.oszk.hu/00900/00979/00239/pdf/1934_39_07-12_261-272.pdf; Visy Zsolt, 'Adatok az 1456 és 1526 közötti török–magyar kapcsolatok megítéléséhez', *Pontes*, Évf. 3 (2020): Határ - Változás – Átmenet, pp. 193–200, https://journals.lib.pte.hu/index.php/pontes/article/view/3394/3173; Cseh Valentin, *A nándorfehérvári csata 1456* (Budapest: Zrínyi Kiadó, 2016)

15 Peter T Leeson, Ennio E Piano, 'The golden age of mercenaries', *European Review of Economic History*, Volume 25, Issue 3, August 2021, pp. 429–446, https://doi.org/10.1093/ereh/heaa020; Kenneth Fowler, 'Sir John Hawkwood and the English Condottieri in Trecento Italy', *Renaissance Studies* Vol. 12, no. 1 (1998): pp. 131–148. http://www.jstor.org/stable/24412633.; Michael Mallett, 'Condottieri' in: Eugenio Garin (ed), *Renaissance Characters* (Chicago: University of Chicago Press, 1997), pp. 22–45; David Murphy, *Condottiere 1300–1500: Infamous medieval mercenaries* (London: Bloomsbury Publishing, 2021); Bárány, Attila. 2002. 'The Communion of English and Hungarian Mercenaries in Italy', in Barta János (ed). *The First Millennium of Hungary in Europe*, pp. 126–141.

16 Ölbei Tamás, 'The Importance of River Valleys in the Overall Strategy of the Mercenary Companies 1357–1366', *British Journal for Military History*, 8.3 (2022), pp. 17–37.

17 Hunt Janin, Ursula Carlson, *Mercenaries in Medieval and Renaissance Europe* (London: McFarland, 2013), pp. 48, 60, 144–145, 148–150, 178–180.; Enikő Csukovits, *Hungary and the Hungarians: Western Europe's View in the Middle Ages* (Rome: Viella Libreria Editrice, 2018), p. 30.; David Murphy, Graham Turner, *Condottiere 1300–1500* (London: Osprey, 2007), pp. 8–12, 26.

18 Janice E. Thomson, *Mercenaries, Pirates and Sovereigns* (Princetown: Princetown University Press, 1994), pp. 32–42.; Edward Cavanagh (2011), 'A Company with Sovereignty and Subjects of Its Own? The Case of the Hudson's Bay Company, 1670–1763', *Canadian journal of law and society*, 26, pp. 25–50 doi:10.3138/cjls.26.1.025; K.H. Wirta, 'Dark horses of business : overseas entrepreneurship in seventeenth-century Nordic trade in the Indian and Atlantic oceans', Doctoral Thesis, Leiden University, 2018, https://scholarlypublications.universiteitleiden.nl/handle/1887/67312; János Besenyő, 'A possible African colony of the Austro-Hungarian Monarchy: Rio de Oro', *Military Historical Bulletins*, Vol. 131, Num. 4, December 2018, pp. 856–884.

19 Ole Feldbæk, 'No Ship to Tranquebar for Twenty-nine Years. Or: The Art of Survival of a Mid Seventeenth Century European Settlement in India', in Ptak and Rothermund (eds), *Emporia, Commodities and Entrepreneurs*, pp. 34–5

20 Alan K. Smith, *Creating a World Economy. Merchant Capital, Colonialism, and World Trade, 1400–1825* (Boulder: Westview Press, 1991), p. 105.

21 C. Tzoref-Ashkenazi, 'German Auxiliary Troops in the British and Dutch East India Companies', in: N. Arielli, B. Collins, (eds) *Transnational Soldiers* (London: Palgrave Macmillan, Clegg, S., 2017), 'The East India Company: The First Modern Multinational?', Multinational Corporations and Organization Theory: *Post Millennium Perspectives* (Research in the Sociology of Organizations, Vol. 49), Emerald Publishing Limited, Bingley, pp. 43–67.

22 Tristan Mostert, *Chain of command. The military system of the Dutch East India Company 1655–1663*, Master´s thesis, Department of History, Research Master of the History of European Expansion and Global Interaction, Universiteit Leiden, June 2007, pp. 20–21; Erik Odegard, 'In search of sepoys: Indian soldiers and the Dutch East India Company in India and Sri Lanka, 1760–1795', *War in History*, Volume 29, Issue 3, pp. 543–562; Kaushik Roy, 'The hybrid military establishment of the East India Company in South Asia: 1750–1849. '*Journal of Global History*, 6(2), pp. 195–218. doi:10.1017/S1740022811000222; Stuart Reid, *Armies of the East India Company 1750–1850* (London: Bloomsbury Publishing, 2012)

23 A. Clulow (2018). 'Great help from Japan: The Dutch East India Company's experiment with Japanese soldiers' in A. Clulow, & T. Mostert (Eds.), *The Dutch and English East India Companies: Diplomacy, Trade and Violence in Early Modern Asia* (Amsterdam University Press, 2018), pp. 179–210.

24 P. Bruce Buchan, 'A Variation on the Origin and Characteristic of the Modern Corporation', *Canadian Journal of Administrative Sciences*, 1995, vol. 12, no. 1, p. 3.

25 Emmet Foley, Christian Kaunert, 'Russian Private Military and Ukraine: Hybrid Surrogate Warfare and Russian State Policy by Other Means', *Central European Journal of International and Security Studies* 16, no. 3 (2022), pp. 172–192, doi: 10.51870/ULJU5827.; Joenniemi: 'Two Models of Mercenarism', pp. 184–196.

26 Fred Halliday, *Mercenaries: 'Counter insurgency' in the Gulf* (Nottingham: Spokesman, 1977), pp. 9–10; Yoel Guzansky and Zachary A. Marshall, 'Outsourcing warfare in the Mediterranean', *Mediterranean Politics* 28, no. 2 (2021), doi: 10.1080/13629395.2021.1924402.; Al J. Venter, Frederick Forsyth, *War Dog. Fighting Other's People Wars. The Modern Mercenary in Combat* (Havertown: Casemate, 2006), pp. 31–32, 247–255, 323–345, 349–351.; Macdonald, *Soldiers of Fortune*, pp. 70–105.; Simon Chesterman, Chia Lehnardt, *From Mercenaries to Market. The Rise and Regulation of Private Military Companies* (New York: Oxford University Press, 2007), pp. 67–81; Abdel-Fatau Musa, J. Kayode Fayemi, *Mercenaries, An African Security Dilemma* (London: Pluto Press, 2000), 265–274; Guy Arnold, *Mercenaries The Scourge of the Third World* (Basingstoke: MacMillan Press Ltd, 1999) pp. 56–64.

27 'Protocols I and II additional to the Geneva Conventions', 8 June 1977, *ICRC homepage*, https://www.icrc.org/en/doc/resources/documents/misc/additional-protocols-1977.htm.

28 *United Nations Treaty Collection*. Chapter XVIII, Penal Matters: International Convention Against the Recruitment, Use, Financing and Training of Mercenaries. United Nations Treaty Collection, 20. October 2001. https://treaties.un.org/Pages/ViewDetails.aspx?src=IND&mtdsg_no=XVIII-6&chapter=18&clang=_en.

29 Scott Fitzsimmons, *Private Security Companies during the Iraq War, Cass Military Studies* (London: Routledge, 2016), p. 43.; Venter, *War Dog*, pp. 555–556.

30 *DCAF Backgrounder: Private Military Companies*, DCAF, April 2006, https://www.files.ethz.ch/isn/17438/backgrounder_09_private-military-companies.pdf, accessed: 19 July 2023.

31 *Private Security Companies*, DCAF, November 2020, https://www.dcaf.ch/sites/default/files/imce/SSAD/Media%20Toolkit/MediaSSR_Toolkit_Tipsheet%2012.pdf, accessed: 19 July 2023.

32 *DCAF Backgrounder: Private Military Companies*, DCAF, April 2006, https://www.files.ethz.ch/isn/17438/backgrounder_09_private-military-companies.pdf, accessed: 19 July 2023.

33 Catalog of Russian PMCs: 37 private military companies of the Russian Federation, Molfar, 2023, https://www.molfar.global/en-blog/catalog-of-russian-pmcs, accessed: 13 July 2023,

34 'Wagner PMC formally non-existent, Putin says — media, The president explained that Russia has no law on private military companies and, therefore, 'there is no such legal entity'', *TASS*, 14 July 2023, https://tass.com/politics/1646675, accessed: 14 July 2023.

35 2009–2010: Xe Services LLC; 2010–2014: Academi; since 2014 part of the Constellis Group; Philippe Chapleau, 'La fusion qui compte: Academi, Triple Canopy s'allient au sein du Constellis Group', *Lignes de Défense Blog*, 11 June 2014, https://lignesdedefense.blogs.ouest-france.fr/archive/2014/06/11/acadeli-triple-canopy-s-allient-pour-former-le-constellis-gr-11976.html, accessed: 9 January 2023.

36 Sean McFate, *Mercenaries and War: Understanding Private Armies Today* (Washington D.C.: National Defense University Press, 2019), pp. 2–8, 18–23; Claire Courtin, 'The transfer of Russian arms to Libya: revealing the Role of private military companies', *Werra*, September 2021, https://en.associationwerra.com/research/research-papers/armaments-industry-and-new-technologies-committee

37 Jordi Palou-Loverdos, Leticia Armendáriz, *The Privatization of Warfare, Violence and Private Military & Security Companies: A factual and legal approach to human rights abuses by PMSC in Iraq* (Nova-Social Innovation Centre, 2011), pp. 34–40.

38 Sergey Sukhankin, 'An Anatomy of the Chinese Private Security Contracting Industry, The Jamestown Foundation', 3 January 2023, https://jamestown.org/program/an-anatomy-of-the-chinese-private-security-contracting-industry/; Spearin, C. (2020). 'China's Private Military and Security Companies: 'Chinese Muscle' and the Reasons for U.S. Engagement', PRISM, 8(4), pp. 40–53. https://www.jstor.org/stable/26918233; Jong Min Lee and Samuel Wittman, 'Will China's Private Security Companies Follow the Wagner Group's Footsteps in Africa?' *The Diplomat*, June 24, 2023, https://thediplomat.com/2023/06/will-chinas-private-security-companies-follow-the-wagner-groups-footsteps-in-africa/, accessed: 9 January 2023.

39 'Private military companies: steady business, as honorable gentlemen', *WeapoNews.com*, 3 July 2020, https://weaponews.com/history/65363941-private-military-companies-steady-business-as-honorable-gentlemen.html.; 'Private military companies: steady business, as honorable gentlemen', *WeapoNews*, 3 July 2020, https://weaponews.com/history/65363941-private-military-companies-steady-business-as-honorable-gentlemen.html, accessed: July 19, 2023.

40 Radwa Ammar, 'Private Military and Security Companies and Regional Security Governance: An interpretive perspective of the United Arab Emirates policies', *Journal of the College of Politics and Economics*, sixth issue - April 2. 2020, pp. 178–210. https://jocu.journals.ekb.eg/article_128643.html; Andreas Krieg (2022) 'The UAE's 'dogs of war': boosting a small state's regional power projection', *Small Wars & Insurgencies*, 33:1–2, pp. 152–172, DOI: 10.1080/09592318.2021.1951432; J. Jezdimirovic Ranito, C.T. Mayer, 'Normalization of mercenary-like private military and security companies: the need for re-securitization of regulation'. Int Polit 58, pp. 772–791 (2021). https://doi.org/10.1057/s41311-020-00271-3; Andreas Krieg (2023) 'Security assistance to surrogates – how the UAE secures its regional objectives', *Mediterranean Politics*, DOI: 10.1080/13629395.2023.2183659

41 Mahmut Cengiz, Layla Hashemi, and Vladimir Semizhanov, 'Alternative Ways to Seek Regional and Global Influence: How Shadowy Organizations Serve the Interests of Turkey, Iran, and Russia', *Small Wars Journal*, 4 July 2022, https://smallwarsjournal.com/jrnl/art/alternative-ways-seek-regional-and-global-influence-how-shadowy-organizations-serve; Fatih Çağatay Cengiz (2020) 'Proliferation of neopatrimonial domination in Turkey', *British Journal of Middle Eastern Studies*, 47:4, pp. 507-525, DOI: 10.1080/13530194.2018.1509693; James Kenneth Wither: 'Outsourcing warfare: Proxy forces in contemporary armed conflicts', *Security and Defence Quarterly*, 31/2020, Issue No. 4, pp. 17–34, https://www.ceeol.com/search/article-detail?id=983355, accessed: 19 July 2023.

42 S. Buchner, (2007), 'Private Military Companies and Domestic Law in South Africa' in: T. Jäger, G. Kümmel (eds) *Private Military and Security Companies* (VS Verlag für Sozialwissenschaften, 2007). https://doi.org/10.1007/978-3-531-90313-2_25; Sabelo Gumedze: Appendix A: List of South African PMCs and PSCs, Monograph No 146, July 2008, https://issafrica.org/appendix-a-list-of-south-african-pmcs-and-pscs; 'The face of the modern mercenary', Africa Defense Forum, 22nd Feb 2022, https://www.defenceweb.co.za/land/land-land/the-face-of-the-modern-mercenary/, accessed: 20 March 2023.

43 'Prigozhin otvetil na vopros ob 'istoshchenii' CHVK 'Vagner'',*Rusvesna* 23 (May 2023), https://rusvesna.su/news/1684840554, accessed: 19 July 2023; 'Operatsiya Z: Voyenkory Russkoy Vesny', *Telegram*, 23 May 2023, https://t.me/RVvoenkor/45636, accessed: 24 May 2023.

44 Andrew Zhang, 'Who is Yevgeny Prigozhin?, The mercenary chief is at the heart of Russia's growing internal strife. Prigozhin reports Rostov military headquarters are under Wagner control', *Politico*, 23 June 2023, https://www.politico.com/news/2023/06/23/yevgeny-prigozhin-russia-ukraine-00103521 accessed: 20 July 2023; Jong Min Lee, Samuel Wittman, 'Will China's Private Security Companies Follow the Wagner Group's Footsteps in Africa?, As the controversial Russian mercenary group is diverting its attention to Ukraine, China's PSCs have a window to expand their engagement in African countries', *The Diplomat*, 24 June 2023, https://thediplomat.com/2023/06/will-chinas-private-security-companies-follow-the-wagner-groups-footsteps-in-africa/, accessed: 19 July 2023.

45 P.K. Balachandran, 'Wagner Group brings spotlight back on mercenary outfits', *Sunday Observer*, 2 July 2023, https://www.sundayobserver.lk/2023/07/02/wagner-group-brings-spotlight-back-mercenary-outfits, accessed: 19 July 2023; Nicolas Camut, Douglas Busvine, 'Wagner troops won't go back to fight in Ukraine, Prigozhin says, 'What is happening at the front now is a disgrace. We want no part of it', mutinous warlord says', *Politico*, 19 July 2023, https://www.politico.eu/article/yevgeny-prigozhin-wagner-troops-russia-ukraine-war-belarus/, accessed: 20 July 2023.

# ABOUT THE AUTHORS

Colonel (Ret.) János Besenyő is a professor in Óbuda University, Hungary, and head of the Africa Research Institute. Between 1987 and 2018, he worked as a professional soldier and served in several peace operations in Africa and Afghanistan. He received a PhD in military science from Zrínyi Miklós National Defense University and a habilitated doctorate at Eötvös Lóránd University. In 2014, he established the Scientific Research Center of the Hungarian Defence Forces General Staff and was its first leader from 2014 to 2018. His most recent publication is *Darfur Peacekeepers: The African Union Peacekeeping Mission in Darfur (AMIS) from the Perspective of a Hungarian Military Advisor*.

András István Türke is director of the Europa Varietas Institute, Switzerland, and senior research fellow of the Africa Research Institute (Óbuda University, Hungary). Between 2006–2011 he worked as visiting fellow at the European Union Institute for Security Studies (EUISS) as well as at the Assembly of the Western European Union - Defence Committee (AWEU). Between 2013–2018 he was lecturer at the University of Szeged, at the Pannon University in Veszprém and at the National University of Public Service (Hungary). Dr. Türke holds a PhD degree in History of International Relations from the Sorbonne University (Paris III EEC-ED385) and received a habilitated doctorate at University of Szeged. His most recent publication is the contemporary history of the Democratic Republic of Congo, Rwanda and Burundi (chapters in a book on French-speaking Africa).

Lieutenant Colonel (Ret.) Endre Szénási is a retired Field Artillery officer and a former strategic analyst of the Hungarian Ministry of Defence. He served as a professional soldier between 1988 and 2023. Following graduation at Kossuth Lajos Military High School (Hungary, 1989), Field Artillery Officers' Advanced Course in the United States of America, Field Artillery Officers' Staff Course (Hungary), he got his Masters' Degree at the Miklós Zrínyi National Defence University (Hungary) receiving a Security- and Defence Policy Expert's diploma in 2022. Between 1989 and 1995 he served at several Field Artillery units in Hungary as a subunit commander. He served as a professional duty officer in Cyprus at the UNFICYP HQ between 1995–1997. He was a senior strategic analyst of the Defence Policy Department of the Hungarian Ministry of Defence between 1997–2023, with multiple fields of expertise stretching from post-soviet policies to global migration, energy security and climate change etc. He retired after 35 years of service as a professional soldier.